MW01609799

Everything You Want to Know

About Acupuncture

By
Tiong-hung Ling, Ph.D.
Nancy T. Ling, Ph.D.

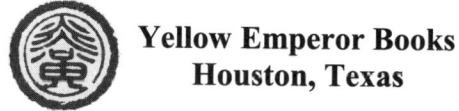

Yellow Emperor Books
Houston, Texas

First Edition, April 2003

Library of Congress Control Number: 2003103236
ISBN 1-59329-000-4

Printed in the United States of America

Yellow Emperor Books
www.YellowEmperorBooks.com

*This book is dedicated to
our father
Rev. Siu-di Ling*

ACKNOWLEDGMENTS

We would like to express our gratitude and thanks to the following persons:

The Rev. Dr. Daniel Hock-ping Ling and Professor Alan Stone of the University of Houston, who read the entire manuscript and made corrections and suggestions; Mrs. Eve Bartlett, who read a section of the first draft and made some corrections; and the editor, Diane Rivera, who spent many hours bringing the book to its final form.

We also thank those patients who have been kind enough to let us use their letters in this book, and many other patients, relatives, and friends who in one way or another assisted in the publication of it.

Finally, we thank those numerous acupuncturists we encountered in China who generously shared valuable experiences and information with us.

PREFACE

Most acupuncture books are written with too much emphasis on acupuncture theory, relevant only to those who have to learn acupuncture. This book is written solely with the lay public in mind and therefore, the style, structure, and content of this book are geared to satisfy the informational needs of that public.

You will notice too that special attempts have been made to trace acupuncture to the ultimate authority—China, where acupuncture was discovered and developed. Due to the fact that very little information about acupuncture is available from China, this book may be helpful to those who want to know exactly what Chinese acupuncture is all about.

We do not intend the information in this book to be used as a substitute for medical treatment or advice. A person feeling ill should seek the counsel of his or her physician.

This book is not written to promote acupuncture or the practical use thereof. Rather its purpose is to provide information so that the reader can see what acupuncture is, what it can do, and what it cannot do. The reader should bear in mind that acupuncture practice is still illegal in many states in the U.S.A.

Tiong-hung Ling
Nancy T. Ling
Peking Acupuncture Clinic

FOREWORD

Acupuncture was originated in China and it can be traced all the way back to the Old Stone Age of the history of China during which time the "bien" (stone acupuncture needle) was used to treat diseases. Though the development of acupuncture art was very slow, the theories and clinical practices had already become quite systematic in the Jin Dynasty, when Huang Fumi (215-282 A.D.) compiled the *Zhenjiu Jia Yi Jing*.

Acupuncture has not only served the people of China for a long time. Without doubt, it was also introduced to Asian countries such as Japan as early as the 6th century and to Europe in the seventeenth century, and it has since been making contributions to the health care of people worldwide.

Dr. Nancy T. Ling and Dr. Tiong-hung Ling have high regard for Chinese acupuncture and China. The acupuncture information that they acquired has made it possible to compile this book, *Everything You Want To Know About Acupuncture*. The book touches some of the most important aspects in acupuncture and can be considered a rather comprehensive introduction to acupuncture. Those viewpoints of their own can also assist the general readers in acquiring a better understanding of what Chinese acupuncture actually is.

The authors met me at the Second National Acupuncture and Moxibustion and Acupuncture Anesthesia Symposium held in Peking, China. I am pleased to be asked to write the foreword for the book. After reading the manuscript, I feel that their ambition and effort are quite admirable, and I feel happy to respond with these few words.

Chen Xingnong
Professor of Acupuncture
International Acupuncture Training Center
Vice President,
National Acupuncture Society of China

TABLE OF CONTENTS

CHAPTER ONE: THEORIES OF ACUPUNCTURE

What is "acupuncture"?
What are the meridians?
What are the Twelve Regular Channels?
What are the Eight Extra Channels?
Why sometimes does one hear about "Fourteen" instead of "Twelve Regular Channels"?
What are the Fifteen Collaterals?
What is an acupoint and when were the major points discovered?
How many acupoints are there?
Which was discovered first, the acupoints or the meridians?
What is the Yin and Yang? theory?
What is the doctrine of Five Elements?
Does the West have something similar to the theory of Yin and Yang?

CHAPTER TWO: SCIENTIFIC ASPECTS OF ACUPUNCTURE

Why did it take so long for the Chinese to make scientific inquiries about acupuncture?
Can acupoints or meridians be seen?
How and under what conditions can meridians be seen by the naked eye?
Can meridians be felt?
Can acupoints be verified?
What do the visibility of meridians, the P.S.M., and the verification of acupoints suggest in the realm of science?
Are there any other scientific breakthroughs?
How does acupuncture work?

CHAPTER THREE: MOXIBUSTION

What is moxibustion?

How old is moxibustion?

What is moxa?

Is it very painful to receive a moxa treatment?

If it was so painful to receive the moxa treatment in ancient times, then why did most people take it?

Is moxa treatment as painful as it was then?

Besides those already mentioned, are there any other ways to administer moxa treatment?

What is a moxa roll?

What are the moxa treatment devices?

Can a cigar or cigarette do the job of a moxa roll?

What is the warm needle method?

Is moxibustion effective?

Since ancient moxibustion was sometimes done with general anesthesia or localized anesthesia, which involved no pain and no feeling, is that not in direct conflict with the nerve aspect just mentioned?

CHAPTER FOUR: DIAGNOSIS IN ACUPUNCTURE

How does an acupuncturist make a diagnosis?

How is pulse taking administered?

Who formulated the four diagnostic procedures?

Is pulse taking as a diagnostic procedure dependable?

Is pulse taking easy to learn?

Are the four diagnostic procedures the only means an acupuncturist uses?

How can the ear be used for diagnosis?

How is ear diagnosis done?

How can the channel theories be applied for diagnosis?

What are some examples?

CHAPTER FIVE: HISTORY OF ACUPUNCTURE

How old is acupuncture?

How old are the oldest acupuncture needles discovered in China?

How could this art that was practiced for so long remain relatively unknown to the world for such a long time?

Did acupuncture enjoy continual acceptance in the course of Chinese history?

Did the ancient Chinese government support acupuncture?

Did the Imperial Medical College make any contributions to the advancement of acupuncture?

Can you give a little more information about the bronze acupuncture models?

Were there any other acupuncture models built after the first two?

Are there any significant models that were built recently?

When did acupuncture encounter its first major setback in China?

Did the Goumindang government promote acupuncture?

What has been the policy of the Chinese government toward acupuncture?

What are some of these significant achievements in acupuncture by the new government?

CHAPTER SIX: DISSEMINATION

In the past, how was acupuncture taught in China?

Besides China, where is acupuncture most popular and how did it start there?

Is Chinese medicine also popular in Japan?

How was acupuncture introduced to Korea?

How was acupuncture introduced to Europe?

How was acupuncture introduced to the West in recent times?

Why is it so difficult for acupuncture to be accepted in the West?

How did acupuncture come to the United States?

In countries where acupuncture is unknown, how would people respond to it?

CHAPTER SEVEN: ACUPUNCTURE ANESTHESIA

When and how was acupuncture anesthesia first introduced?

Did acupuncture anesthesia gain widespread use in China immediately after its introduction?

Are the acupoints used for anesthesia altogether different from regular acupoints?

Where are the needles inserted for acupuncture anesthesia?

How many needles are used in acupuncture anesthesia?

Can acupuncture anesthesia be employed for open heart surgery?

Are there any advantages in using acupuncture anesthesia instead of the anesthetic drug?

What are some of the advantages of acupuncture anesthesia?

Are there any disadvantages of acupuncture anesthesia?

CHAPTER EIGHT: CLINICAL POTPOURRI

What can acupuncture do?

Is acupuncture treatment good for any kind of disease?

How is the acupuncture needle inserted?

Is the guide tube method better?

How many needles are usually used for a treatment?

Is it better to have more needles used or less needles used?

Is the use of fewer points or fewer needles considered an improved method or a more modern technique?

Is any kind of drug applied on the needles?

Can acupuncture patients get different results from different acupuncturists?

Will different acupuncturists achieve different results even though they use the same acupoints prescribed to treat a given ailment?

Do all acupuncturists prescribe the same acupoints for a given disease?

Is there an acupuncturist who is capable of listing all the acupoint prescriptions for all the known treatable ailments?

What are the reasons?

Do the Chinese keep trade secrets?

Do most of the achievements in acupuncture or Chinese medicine come easily?

Is there any place on the body where an acupuncture needle should not be inserted?

When is it best to have acupuncture treatment?

Should a patient observe any restrictions after an acupuncture treatment?

Is there any pain involved when an acupuncture needle is being inserted?

Can the level of pain experienced from needle insertion be different with different acupuncturists?

Can an acupuncture needle break inside the body?

Can one take acupuncture treatment at any time?

Is acupuncture treatment dangerous?

Can some minor accidents occur under acupuncture treatment?

Does acupuncture treatment work for everyone every time?

Why do some people sometimes not respond to acupuncture treatment or respond poorly?

Some people will faint while receiving an injection or while donating blood. Can this happen to these same people while they are receiving acupuncture treatment?

Is there any danger if this happens?

Since more women than men are afraid of needles, are women more apt to feel dizzy?

Are there some acupoints that tend to cause dizziness more than others?

Why should a person not take an acupuncture treatment if he or she is too hungry or too full?

Can more than one ailment be treated at the same time?

What treatment intervals are most realistic and economical?

How deep are the acupuncture needles inserted?

How soon after an acupuncture treatment can one expect results?

Can acupuncture treatment be used for birth control?

Can acupuncture be used for abortion?

Can acupuncture treatment be used to prevent the flu?

Is acupuncture helpful for attaining longevity?

Can acupuncture treatment help to prevent stroke?

CHAPTER ONE
Theories of Acupuncture

What Is "Acupuncture"?

"Acupuncture" is a word made up of the Latin word "acus," which means needle, and the English word "puncture." The general term for acupuncture in Chinese is "zhenjiu." "Zhen" is the art of needling while "jiu" means moxibustion, or heat treatment. In Chinese, both words are always used together to mean acupuncture. However, when the term was translated into English, only the first half of the meaning was used. Thus, the term acupuncture is actually misleading because it fails to include moxibustion, the other half of the treatment involved.

Acupuncture treatment involves the use of needles and/or moxibustion (the burning of a cone of dried artemisia vulgaris on acupoints) for the prevention and treatment of diseases. This method was discovered and developed by the Chinese, and it has a history that is several thousand years old. The application of these needles and/or moxa to certain points on the body can produce specific functional changes that can achieve certain therapeutic results. Sometimes the treatment is done with needles only, sometimes with moxa only, and at other times with both or with one after the other. The needles or moxa are not simply applied anywhere on the body but are applied mostly at specific body points known as acupoints. These acupoints have been identified along many pathways (known as meridians) in and on the body. Because the part of the word that means moxibustion was omitted from the English translation of the term acupuncture, some writers have begun to refer to both "acupuncture and moxibustion" instead of just "acupuncture." This solves one problem but creates another one because it defines with two separate terms a procedure the Chinese have always considered as one. The semantic problem has existed right from the beginning but has never been challenged. As the West learns more about acupuncture, or more particularly, moxibustion, the problem will be more apparent. Except for some authors who have tried to correct the mistake by using "moxibustion" with the term "acupuncture," no attempt has ever been made to resolve this problem.

For the sake of clarity and simplicity, in this book we will use the term "acupuncture" to mean both "acupuncture and moxibustion." The Chinese have a proverb that says "if a mistake is repeated forever, it is no longer a mistake." Perhaps then, it is better to add the meaning of moxibustion to the existing term acupuncture even though it is semantically incorrect.

What Are The Meridians?

Meridians are definite pathways in and on the body through which "Qi" (pronounced "chi"), or life energy, travels. The major pathways connect the internal organs and traverse outward to link with the extremities, which lay on the exterior of the body. Some of the minor pathways link the major pathways together while others branch out to reach almost anywhere on the body. All pathways are systematically linked to form a closed circuit with definite directions through which "Qi" travels.

There are three main groups of pathways, with two other groups that are seldom mentioned. The three main groups are the Twelve Regular Channels, the Eight Extra Channels, and the Fifteen Major Collaterals.

What Are The Twelve Regular Channels?

The Twelve Regular Channels, also known as "jing" by the Chinese, are:

(1) The Lung Channel of Hand-Taiyin.
(2) The Large Intestine Channel of Hand-Yangming.
(3) The Stomach Channel of Foot-Yangming.
(4) The Spleen Channel of Foot-Taiyin.
(5) The Heart Channel of Hand-Shaoyin.
(6) The Small Intestine Channel of Hand-Taiyang.
(7) The Urinary Bladder Channel of Foot-Taiyang.
(8) The Kidney Channel of Foot-Shaoyin.
(9) The Pericardium Channel of Hand-Jueyin.
(10) The Sanjiao Channel of Hand-Shaoyang
(11) The Gall Bladder Channel of Foot-Shaoyang.
(12) The Liver Channel of Foot-Jueyin.

What Are The Eight Extra Channels?

Most of the Eight Extra Channels are branches of the Twelve Regular Channels. These eight channels serve as connectors for the Twelve Regular Channels. The Eight Extra Channels are:

(1) The Du Channel.
(2) The Ren Channel.
(3) The Chong Channel.
(4) The Dai Channel.
(5) The Yangqiao Channel.
(6) The Yinqiao Channel.
(7) The Yangwei Channel.
(8) The Yinwei Channel.

Why Sometimes Does One Hear About "Fourteen" Instead of "Twelve Regular Channels"?

Among the Eight Extra Channels, the Du and Ren Channels are more important than the others in that group, and both have characteristics of the Twelve Regular Channels. Therefore, these two channels are sometimes added to the Twelve Regular Channels to make Fourteen Regular Channels.

What Are The Fifteen Collaterals?

Each of the previously mentioned Fourteen Regular Channels possesses one collateral. Thus there will be fourteen collaterals plus an extra collateral of the spleen, making fifteen in all.

I. General Illustration on Courses of the channels

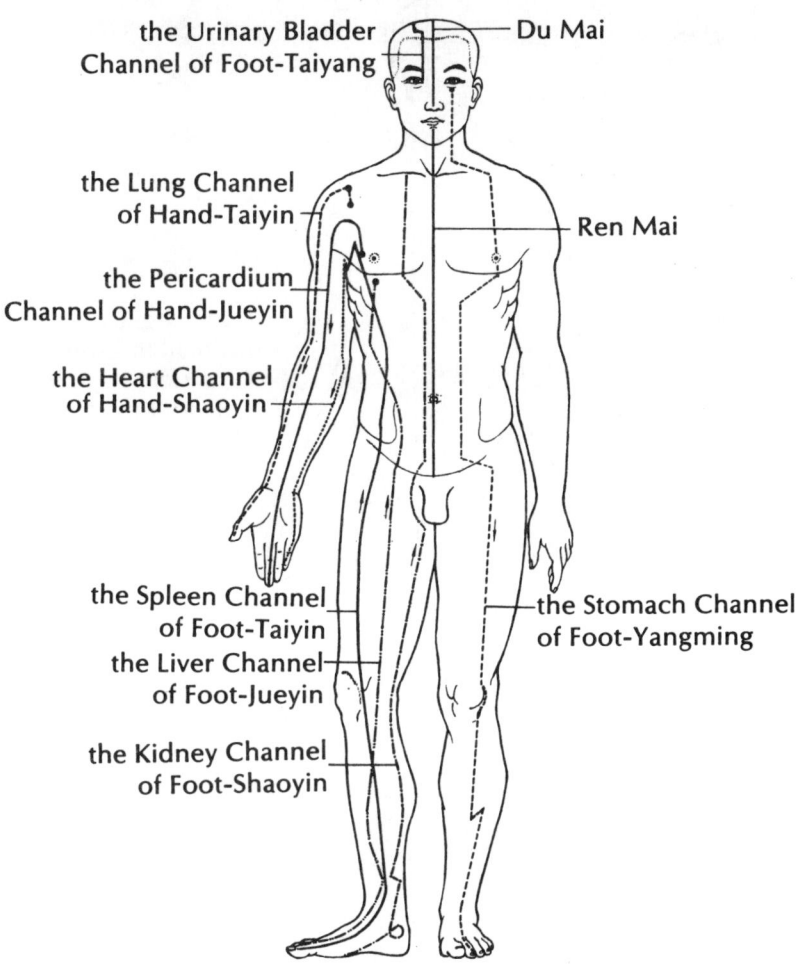

the Urinary Bladder
Channel of Foot-Taiyang

Du Mai

the Lung Channel
of Hand-Taiyin

Ren Mai

the Pericardium
Channel of Hand-Jueyin

the Heart Channel
of Hand-Shaoyin

the Spleen Channel
of Foot-Taiyin

the Stomach Channel
of Foot-Yangming

the Liver Channel
of Foot-Jueyin

the Kidney Channel
of Foot-Shaoyin

Fig. 1   Distribution of Fourteen Channels (Anterior View)

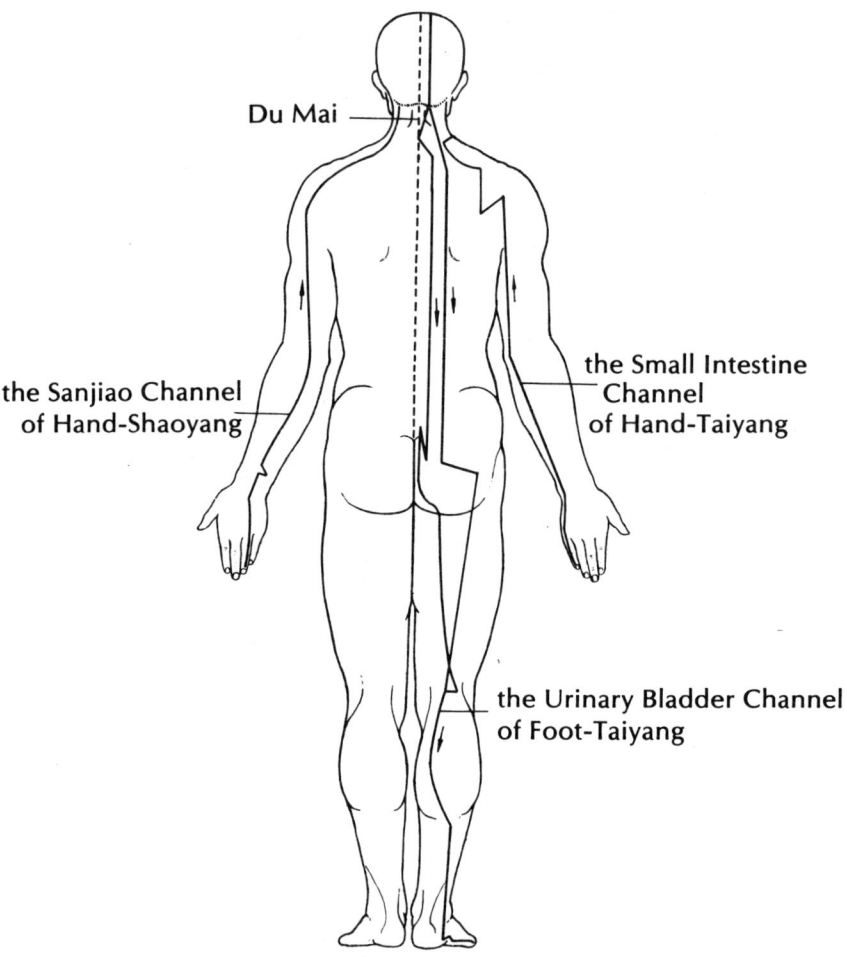

Fig. 2 Distribution of Fourteen Channels (Posterior View)

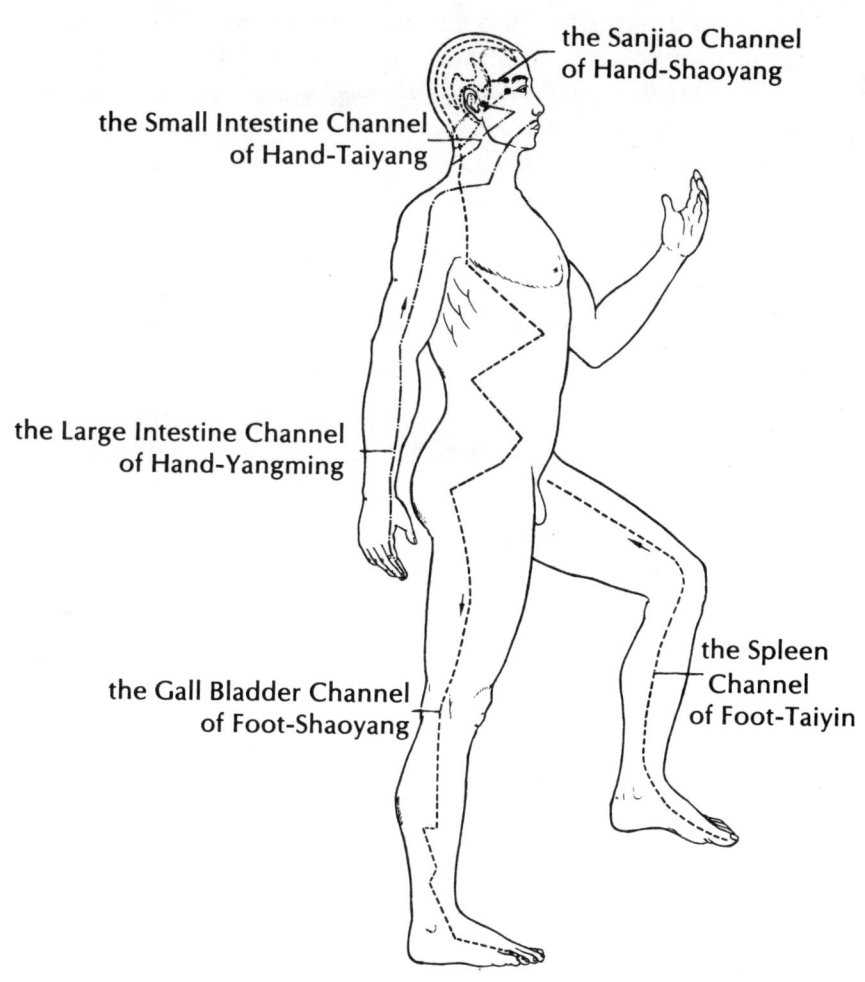

the Sanjiao Channel
of Hand-Shaoyang

the Small Intestine Channel
of Hand-Taiyang

the Large Intestine Channel
of Hand-Yangming

the Spleen
Channel
of Foot-Taiyin

the Gall Bladder Channel
of Foot-Shaoyang

Fig. 3 Distribution of Fourteen Channels (Side View)

What Is An Acupoint and When Were The Major Points Discovered?

An acupoint is a specific spot on the body where needling or moxibustion can be administered in order to bring about an intended therapeutic effect. These specific spots exist in all human beings, regardless of race or sex. When a needle is inserted in that specific spot or when moxibustion is applied to the spot, functional reactions by certain organs of the body or changes of the viscera will occur.

Before these spots were defined as acupoints, many trial and error experiments must have been undertaken, involving hundreds of years of research and study.

The book *Neijing* lists 295 acupoints. After some 2,000 years of further exploration, experimentation, and application, these 295 points remain by and large unchallenged. In practical terms, this means that even 2,000 years ago, the Chinese had already reached such an advanced stage in defining acupoints that they left little room for improvement. Today, we can use electronic devices to verify the existence of the already discovered acupoints. However, these devices cannot challenge the earlier work of the ancient Chinese. They discovered not only the acupoints but also most of the functions of these points that yield indications for therapy.

How Many Acupoints Are There?

This question is often asked, and the answers given vary so much that one may wonder whether answers with greater numbers of acupoints reflect superiority. Of course, this conjecture has no validity at all. The *Neijing,* compiled between 403 and 221 B.C., listed 295 acupoints. In *Jiayijing*, another book on acupuncture compiled in

256 A.D., 349 points were listed. This means that from *Neijing* to *Jiayijing,* 54 acupoints were added. *Zhenjiu Fengyuan,* compiled in 1817 A.D., listed 361 acupoints. Thus, only 12 new acupoints were discovered and added in the 1,561 years from *Jiayijing* to *Zhenjiu Fengyuang.* From 1817 A.D. to 1900, still not too many more acupoints were added. During the last 50 years, however, by far the greatest number of acupoints have been identified and added to the list. So far, in all books on acupuncture published in Mainland China, there are just over 1,600 different acupoints listed, and this is already considered by some as almost reaching the saturation point. One book published in Taiwan in 1976 lists 2,001 acupoints. We should point out that over the last 2,000 years, the number of acupoints found along the Fourteen Regular Channels has remained almost the same. Most of the new acupoints that have been identified and added to the list have been found on the Extra Channels only. Futhermore, it is neither easy nor necessary for an acupuncturist to remember more than 200 to 300 acupoints, and in fact, few acupuncturists can remember more than 400.

Which Was Discovered First, The Acupoints Or The Meridians?

It looks likely for either one to beget the other. Until the last decade or so, most acupuncture theorists and writers tended to agree that acupoints came first. But since the early 1970s, this theory has faced an unprecedented challenge. The challenge has come from two important discoveries.

(1) In 1973, the Han Tomb III in Mawangdui, Hunan Province, was discovered. Four medical books were excavated together with some other relics. These books were written during the Three Warring States, when

Neijing was also written. What is important is that one of the four books mentions only 11 meridians instead of 12 according to *Neijing*. Furthermore, the absence in these books of any mention of acupoints seems to confirm that the meridians had an earlier origin than did the acupoints. This discovery not only challenges the theory that acupoints existed first but it also questions the claim that *Neijing* is the oldest medical book.

(2) The sighting of meridians on the human body makes it comprehensible and possible that the ancient Chinese sighted and discovered the meridians before they found the acupoints.

What Is The Yin and Yang Theory?

Like acupuncture, the Yin-Yang school of thought was already in existence over 2,000 years ago, and its origin is just impossible to trace. Tsou Yen (305-204 B.C.) is considered the earliest chief exponent of the theory and was the first scholar to incorporate the Yin-Yang theory and the Doctrine of the Five Elements.

The Yin-Yang theory presupposes that everything is under constant change, either moving toward "becoming" or toward "disintegration." There is no absolute tranquility. Even things that seem to be tranquil still embrace change in slow motion or in a hidden guise. This constant change being driven by the forces or powers of Yin-Yang can be described in three categories:

(1) Yin-Yang are both contradictory and interdependent. The existence of one depends on the existence of and interplay with the other. That is, Yin or Yang could never exist separately in isolation. It is exactly this contradiction that brings motion and livelihood to Yin-Yang in a mutual coexisting unity.

(2) Yin-Yang have the nature of mutual transfiguration, which results from the continuous interaction and contradiction of both. This not only is essential for survival but it also enables the entity to evolve in constant change. Sometimes either the Yin or Yang may split or one may encompass the other. At other times, one will significantly transfuse into the other or transform the other.

(3) The mutual diminution and restitution is part of the Yin-Yang interplay; one seeks to diminish or transfigure the other. The loser makes restitution, which becomes the winner's gain.

There are very few ancient Chinese classic books that can be considered completely free from the Yin-Yang influence. The theory was and is present in philosophy, medicine, art, government, and many other aspects of the Chinese lifestyle. In fact, the theory is so pervasive in Chinese culture that very few Chinese have escaped its influence in one way or another. For example, in most major undertakings such as the building of a house—or even the selection of burial sites—dates and locations are carefully selected by experts so as to take all the advantages that nature can provide. On the other side of the coin, ill-chosen dates or locations can offend nature and, therefore, invite trouble. Many people in China still observe these practices closely while the Chinese living in other countries tend to ignore them.

In the American culture, an example of this would be "Friday the 13th" or the number "13," which are considered unlucky.

It is from the Yin and Yang theory that the Chinese formulated a common law that governs both man and nature. This law states that human beings live in nature and that their lives and destinies are affected by it. However, human beings can also change the nature that affects them. This mutual interplay between human beings and nature is explained in the *Doctrine of Means,* which says: When a nation or family is about to flourish, lucky omens will precede the event. If they should be about to perish, unlucky omens will precede the happening.

What Is The Doctrine of Five Elements?

The Doctrine of Five Elements presupposes that the universe is basically made up of five elements: wood, fire, earth, metal, and water. A Chinese scholar, Hsun Tzu (298-238 B.C.) mentioned that Tzu-Ssu (492-431 B.C.), a grandson of Confucius, made efforts to improve the Doctrine of Five Elements and that this work was later carried on by Mencius, another scholar. But strangely enough, the Doctrine of Five Elements was mentioned or used least in the Confucius-Mencius classics. One possible reason for this could be that volumes by these scholars pertaining to this doctrine were lost.

The Doctrine of Five Elements takes for granted that everything in the universe—whether it is tangible or otherwise—comes from the interaction of the Five Elements, driven by a pair of Yin and Yang forces. The reality of existence is always dynamic and is never static, and the outcome is a continuous becoming through transfiguration. Transfiguration is manifested in an orderly manner rather than in a chaotic one. Of course, the essence of the Doctrine of Five Elements is motion of the elements rather than the tangible elements themselves.

There are two major categories under which the working order of the Five Elements can be described.

(1) Mutual begetting: wood begets fire, fire begets earth, earth begets metal, metal begets water, and water in turn begets wood.

(2) Mutual supressing: wood suppresses earth, earth suppresses water, water suppresses fire, fire suppresses metal, and metal in turn suppresses wood.

The Chinese discovered that the theory of Yin-Yang and the Doctrine of Five Elements explained well the phenomena of the physiological and pathological inter-relation of organs of the human body. This unique discovery has become the backbone and guidepost of Chinese medicine, through which the pathology, diagnosis, and treatments of Chinese intrinsic medicine (the traditional Chinese medicine and acupuncture) are formulated and developed.

Some people with scientific minds may at first glance find the doctrines of Yin-Yang and the Five Elements to be illogical or absurd. Comprehension can help to reverse this attitude.

Does The West Have Something Similar To The Theory of Yin and Yang?

Yes, there is a Western counterpart, although it is not precisely identical to the Yin-Yang theory. This is known as the Hegelian Dialectic, founded by the German philosopher Georg Hegel (1770-1831 A.D.) The Hegelian Dialectic is also a philosophical method of inquiry. It is a principle that describes the movement and activity in the universe. According to Hegel, all reality is developed through the continuous process of contradiction from level to level. This is called the dialectical movement.

In a dialectical movement, the contradictions never reach a state of equilibrium because the process of interaction or contradiction usually results in incompati-bility. This incompatibility always leads to negation of the weaker entity; thus, a new entity is created.

In a dialectical movement, the two opposites are described as the thesis and antithesis. The negation of the weaker of these leads to a new entity called the synthesis. The synthesis in turn becomes the thesis in a new dialectical movement. In the negation process, the unity of the two opposites does not presuppose the complete annihilation of one. One of the two will subsist in abeyance. After the union, it will actually still exist, but in a modified form.

However, because negation of the negation is also unavoidable, change in the dialectical process can be so dramatic that each dialectic process can result in a new vitality and can thereby create an entity very different from its predecessors.

In the Yin-Yang interaction process, the Yin or Yang can split or one can transfuse into the other or transform the other. But the Yin or Yang maintains its original nature even though great changes take place.

In the Chinese Yin-Yang theory, both human beings and nature are important, and the ultimate goal is to seek a changeable but otherwise adaptable unity of human beings and nature. In the Hegelian Dialectic, however, the development of an idea is the ultimate goal, and human beings are considered only the instrument with which to develop the ultimate idea.

In the doctrine of Dialectical Materialism, Karl Marx and Fredrich Engels replaced the "idea" in the Hegelian Dialectic with "materialism." It should be noted that the important role the human being has in the Yin-Yang theory is not found in either the Hegelian Dialectic or the doctrine of Dialectical Materialism.

CHAPTER TWO
Scientific Aspects of Acupunture

Why Did It Take So Long For The Chinese To Make Scientific Inquiries About Acupuncture?

On the whole, the Chinese people may be a little bit less scientifically inclined, that is, slower to move toward science and scientific investigation. The Chinese have had the patience to wrestle with the theories of metaphysics for centuries, but when they first encountered science, they could not be patient long enough to see how science could benefit them. That is why the very first railroad built in China was intentionally demolished and dumped into the sea.

Until just a few decades ago, there was almost no evidence about acupuncture that could be considered presentable for scientific scrutiny. The Chinese, who had practiced acupuncture for a long time, were satisfied with having discovered something that works, and they were not at all concerned with the "why" and "how" of acupuncture. It was not until very recent times that they began to look into the scientific aspects of acupuncture. During the past two decades, most colleges of traditional Chinese medicine in China have in one way or another initiated some research programs in that regard. They have now begun to search for scientific foundations through which acupuncture can be presented in a way that does not offend the modern methods of inquiry.

Can Acupoints Or Meridians Be Seen?

Acupoints cannot be seen, although they can be detected by electronic devices. Meridians normally cannot be seen either, but once in a blue moon, they may be visible if you are lucky enough to see them. Until 1949, it was thought that meridians could never be seen, but in that year, there were reports in Japan that meridians had been sighted on the human body. There was another sighting the following year, again in Japan, when an electric stimulator was connected to acupuncture needles that were inserted in a patient. These sightings by the Japanese were immediately followed by reports about meridian sightings in China, beginning in the early 1950s. At about the same time, a Chinese medical team sent to Africa also reported sighting meridians on African patients.

How And Under What Conditions Can Meridians Be Seen By The Naked Eye?

Most sightings of meridians have been reported after patients were treated with acupuncture, at which time red or white striations, or bleeding bands, occurred along the meridians. In some cases, skin diseases have developed along the meridians. So far, all the 14 major meridians have been sighted under one of these circumstances. Almost 100 pictures illustrating visibility of the 14 major meridians under different situations were on display during the Second National Acupuncture Symposium held in Peking in 1984.

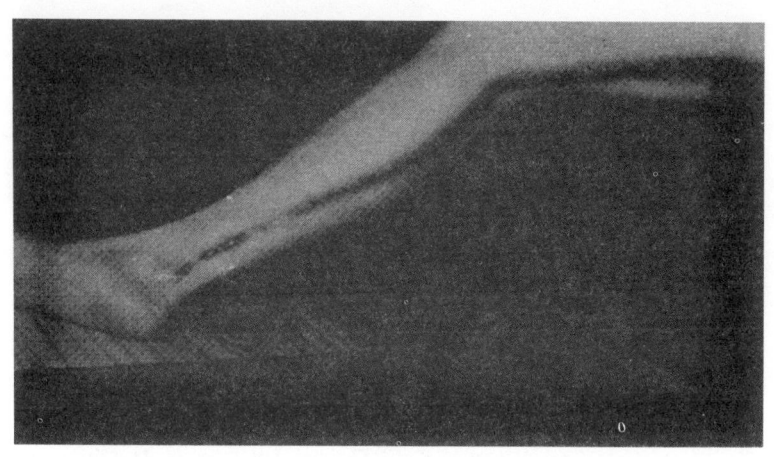

Secondary Neurodematitis that occurred along the right kidney meridian (Wang, female, 29), 1980.

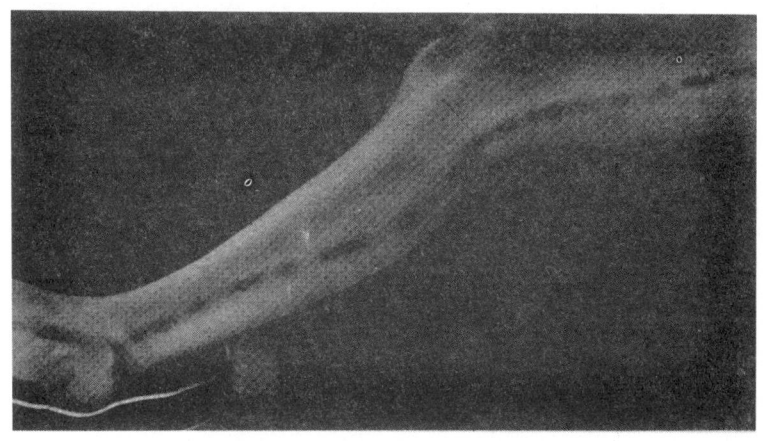

Eczema that occurred along a right kidney meridian (Qian, female, 15), 1980.

Can Meridians Be Felt?

Yes, they can. After the sighting of meridians was reported, Chinese acupuncturists watched for them diligently, but they subsequently found that the chances of actually seeing meridians on the body were really very slim indeed. However, they did discover that needle treatment can also induce propagated sensation along meridians (P.S.M.). When a needle is inserted into the body, sometimes it can induce a distinct sensation that travels consistently along particular lines that coincide with those of the meridians. The best chance to encounter this phenomenon can be achieved by inserting needles on the Jing acupoints on each of the 12 meridians with an electric stimulator hookup. This generated so much interest among Chinese acupuncturists that an intensive nationwide search program to study this unusual phenomenon was launched in 1972. The program, which took 7 years to complete, was carried out by over 30 teams scattered all over China. Of 48,198 persons who were tested for such a phenomenon, 226 were found to be responsive. The likelihood of encountering such an effect was about four persons per thousand. It was also reported that the occurrence rate of this phenomenon was slightly higher among the Africans tested than it was among the Chinese.

Can Acupoints Be Verified?

Yes. In 1950, Nakatani of Tokyo University initiated a study to examine electrical conductivity on human skin. That careful examination identified 370 points on the human body that have one thing in common—low electrical resistance. When the researcher connected these points to form lines that he called "ryodoraku," he was surprised to discover that the "ryodoraku" were identical to the acupuncture meridians found in the book of *Neijing*.

After Nakatani's initial finding, numerous similar investigations were conducted in China, Japan, and the West, and all confirmed his finding.

What Do The Visibility of Meridians, The P.S.M., and The Verification of Acupoints Suggest in The Realm of Science?

The visibility of meridians, the P.S.M., and the verification of acupoints all suggest the possibility of the existence of neural pathways on the human body and the possibility that these presumed neural pathways coincide with the meridians of Chinese acupuncture. Because of these and other findings, for the first time in history modern science is being used in the defense of acupuncture.

Are There Any Other Scientific Breakthroughs?

Yes. One of the important breakthroughs was reported by Professor Han Jisheng of Beijing Medical College. Professor Han was one of the first people to be involved in research on the principles of acupuncture anesthesia. Twenty years of continuous hard work led him and his research group to produce more than 100 papers on the principles of acupuncture anesthesia, which also included some scientific breakthroughs. One of Professor Han's most important contributions was his discovery that a rabbit being treated with acupuncture anesthesia can produce a natural analgesic substance in the cerebro-spinal fluid. If this is drawn from the treated rabbit and injected into another rabbit, the untreated rabbit can also experience the effect of anesthesia. Professor Han and his research group also identified the 5-hydroxylamine and endorphin contents in the central nervous system as important chemical elements in achieving acupuncture analgesia. However, the researchers also discovered that catecholamine and other antiopiate substances produced by acupuncture treatments have antianalgesic effects. These discoveries answer many questions concerning acupuncture anesthesia as they provide scientific explanations revealing how acupuncture anesthesia works.

How Does Acupuncture Work?

This is one of the most frequently asked questions, and there is no single answer that is universally accepted. According to the Chinese acupuncture theory, "Qi" (pronounced "chi") is the key word that explains "how" and "why" acupuncture works. "Qi," or life energy, is invisible and immeasurable. This life energy is driven by Yin and Yang forces to every part of the body through channels called meridians. When there is a free flow of this life energy in the body, there is perfect health. However, if the interplay of the Yin and Yang forces is interrupted or is thrown off balance, then problems will occur or ailments will find their way into the body.

Acupuncture treatments have the capability of returning the energy flow to the normal condition. They can thereby eliminate problems or ailments. But anything that cannot be seen, heard, felt, or measured is very likely to be considered metaphysical. Like some other things in acupuncture theory, the concept of "Qi" is not something that can be easily understood by everyone. People with scientific backgrounds may find it especially difficult to accept the "Qi" explanation and perhaps because it is not strictly scientific, they sometimes react to it with anger, for which the Chinese word is also "Qi." So you can say, whether you like it or not, it is "Qi" after all!

In the last few decades, the Chinese have tried diligently to identify the principles by which acupuncture works. The following findings may offer some clues as one looks for satisfactory answers.

(1) In China, numerous experiments have been conducted on rabbits, rats, and cats to determine whether acupuncture treatments affect the various brain functions. During the Second National Acupuncture Symposium held in 1984, there were more than a hundred papers presented on this topic. All those papers in one way or another reveal that acupuncture treatments do affect brain functions in various ways.

(2) Experiments done on both rabbits and human beings show that needling on the Zusanli point slows down peristalsis of the stomach and that needling on the Shousanli point produces the reverse result. Palpitation of the heart can easily be controlled by acupuncture treatment. These are some examples that demonstrate the possible use of acupuncture to return organ function to normal.

(3) Experiments done in China and reports presented at the Second National Acupuncture Symposium indicated that acupuncture treatments also affect the biochemistry of the body. It was observed that needling at the Zusanli acupoint on a rabbit increases the adrenalin secretion.

(4) Since 1955, Wang Fuzhou and many other researchers in China have conducted experiments on rabbits to determine whether needle treatment on the Zusanli acupoint affects the immune system. All researchers discovered that acupuncture treatment can affect cell activity. It can raise antibody levels by as much as two to three times in just two to three hours after treatment, and the elevated antibody levels are maintained for two to three days, after which time they will return to normal.

(5) There is little doubt that acupuncture treatment has much to do with the neural system of the body. Many attempts have been made to insert needles on paralyzed limbs of patients to achieve functional adjustments and these attempts generated no apparent result. Li Jialing of the Chinese Academy of Medical Sciences, Beijing, has also discovered that electro-acupuncture given to a dog on the Zusanli acupoint can increase sympatho-adrenal secretion while the same treatment given to a dog under anesthesia cannot produce similar results. All these suggest that if acupuncture treatment is rendered where there is no sensation of feeling at all, no response will be forthcoming. The key factor here is nerve response.

CHAPTER THREE
Moxibustion

What Is Moxibustion?

Moxibustion is a treatment procedure in which the moxa herb takes the place of acupuncture needles. The Chinese word for acupuncture is "zhenjiu," which literally means "needling and moxibustion." So moxibustion is actually one kind of acupuncture treatment or part of an acupuncture treatment. It is administered through the burning of a small cone of moxa herb directly on the acupoint.

How Old Is Moxibustion?

Like acupuncture, moxa treatment is very old also and can be traced back to the prehistoric Chinese culture. This treatment probably started soon after the discovery of fire, which led to the subsequent discovery of applying heat for treatment.

The earliest mention of moxibustion is found in the book *Zuo Chuan* in association with the illness of Emperor Jin Jing Gong in 581 B.C. The doctor who examined the Emperor said that his illness was not treatable by existing methods, that is, by moxibustion, acupuncture, or herb.

Over 2,000 years ago, moxa was identified to be the best herb for moxibustion. It was also established that older moxa could yield better treatment results than a fresh one could. A treatise written by Mencius (372-289 B.C.) even advised that "in treating a disease seven years old, use three-year-old moxa."

What Is Moxa?

Moxa is a kind of herb known as artemisia vulgaris, or sagebrush. The leaves of this plant are dried and then ground almost into a powder form when it is ready for use. The volatile oil of the leaves produces a unique aroma, and burning a cone of moxa on an acupoint is capable of producing therapeutic stimulations on the body, through which the treatment result is achieved. According to Wan Xuetai's *Handbook of Acupuncture* (1974), the ingredients of moxa can be broken down as follows:

(1) (Cineol) $C_{10}H_{18}O$ dissolved with Sesquiterpen and Sesquiterpen alcohol
(2) (Artenisin) $C_{10}H_{16}O$
(3) (Adenine) $C_5H_5N_5$
(4) (Choline)) $C_5H_{15}O_2N$
(5) Hentviacontane $C_{31}H_{64}$; Tricosanol $C_{23}H_{48}O$
(6) Wax
(7) Vitamins A, B, C, D

Is It Very Painful To Receive A Moxa Treatment?

Those who are fearful of the minor pain incurred with an acupuncture treatment should be aware of the kind of pain the Chinese people of ancient times had to endure when they received moxa treatments. Until four or five hundred years ago, moxa treatments were done almost exclusively by using the direct scorching or scarring method. This is done by placing a small cone of moxa herb directly on the skin (at the acupoint) and then igniting the cone and letting it burn down to the skin. The pain might be equal to that of burning the skin with a lighted cigarette. The smallest cone is about the size of a wheat grain and the large ones can be as big as a piece of popcorn. There is certainly a lot of pain associated with this treatment. Ancient Chinese historical records have revealed some of the problems that existed, such as "how to convince people to endure the pain during the treatment." A famous figure in ancient times said, "I can tolerate all kinds of pain except moxibustion." This is a clear indication that in ancient times some people were reluctant to take the treatment because of the pain involved.

If It Was So Painful To Receive The Moxa Treatment In Ancient Times, Then Why Did Most People Take It?

When these people got sick, they had few choices in the kind of treatment available to them. This alone might have forced many to take the treatment despite the pain involved. Besides this, there were several methods available to alleviate the pain. One method the Chinese used was a sedative drug known as Suitsensan, which was taken orally. This drug was capable of inducing general anesthesia while the scorching treatment was being administered. Of course, this was used only for those who could not endure the pain. A second method used to alleviate pain was to depress the acupoint quite forcefully just before placing the moxa cone on it and then to further depress around the burning moxa cone. This method, although much less effective than the first one, was very widely used. Later, during the Ming Dynasty (1368-1644 A.D.), a third method was mentioned in the book *Past and Present Medicine*. This remedy involved rubbing a special kind of drug externally on the acupoint to achieve localized anesthesia before the moxa treatment. The book also gave instructions for the preparation of this localized anesthetic drug. Although this method was very helpful, just how widely it was used is not known since it was seldom mentioned in the Chinese medical classics.

Besides herbal medicine, acupuncture and moxibustion were the only treatment methods available to the Chinese in ancient times. If the doctor felt that moxibustion was the only suitable treatment method for certain diseases, then it was either moxibustion or no treatment at all.

Is Moxa Treatment As Painful Now As It Was Then?

By no means. During the Ming Dynasty (1368-1644 A.D.) and in the early part of the Qing Dynasty (1644-1911 A.D.), a new method for administering the moxa treatment emerged out of necessity. This method eliminated the direct scorching by placing something between the moxa and the skin, thus allowing the moxa heat to radiate to the skin while reducing the scorching pain to a tolerable level. The idea of placing the moxa cone on top of something else encouraged almost all acupuncture practitioners to seek out every possible herb or spice that could be placed under the moxa cone. In the several hundred years since this discovery, about forty kinds of spices or herbs have been tested and used. The most popular ones are ginger and garlic slices.

Besides Those Already Mentioned, Are There Any Other Ways To Administer Moxa Treatments?

Yes, there are. The achievement of successful moxa treatment without scorching pain led to the discovery of other ways to administer the treatments. Most of these new methods attempt to reduce heat transmission to the skin either by keeping the burning moxa just close enough to the skin to allow the heat to be felt or by placing something between the moxa cone and the skin. For the former methods, a variety of moxa rolls were invented and for the latter ones, some moxa treatment devices were used. A few other methods did away with the moxa and heat altogether. All these were designed to reduce pain during the treatments.

What Is A Moxa Roll?

After it was discovered that scorching pain and scarring were not essential to the moxa treatment, the necessity to move burning moxa away from the skin when it became too hot to bear led to the invention of the moxa roll. Instead of placing the moxa cone directly on the skin, the burning moxa roll can be hand held close enough to heat the skin but not burn it.

The moxa roll, slightly larger than a cigar, was made from moxa and other herbs. During the Ming and Qing dynasties, all these different kinds of moxa rolls were given different names as different kinds of herbs were also mixed with the moxa. The major kinds were: (a) thunder-fire needle, mostly used for arthritis treatment, (b) tai-yi needle, for general use, and (c) san-chi combination needle, also for general purposes.

Today, the moxa rolls are mostly made from moxa only and they are very widely used. The thunder-fire needle, the tai-yi needle, and the san-chi combination needle are seldom used.

What Are The Moxa Treatment Devices?

The necessity to move the burning moxa cone away from the skin led to the improvisation of devices that could both do the job and conveniently be used. About ten kinds of moxa treatment devices were invented. Most were small cup-type containers or flat objects with a hole in the center (few had more than one hole) upon which a moxa cone slightly larger than the hole was placed. In a moxa treatment, the device was placed next to the skin or close to it, with the moxa cone burning just above the acupoint. The ancient Chinese copper coin, with a square hole in the center, was also used as a device. All these devices allowed better control of heat transmission to the skin and, therefore, made the treatment much less painful to endure. Today, most are obsolete and therefore have become collector's items.

Can A Cigar or Cigarette Do The Job of A Moxa Roll?

Some years ago, experiments were conducted in China to find out whether a cigarette or cigar could take the place of a moxa roll. The results were all negative.

What Is The Warm Needle Method?

This is a unique acupuncture treatment technique known to have been used first by the Chu people in China. It became better known and was adopted as a treatment method during the Ming Dynasty (1386-1644 A.D.). The method, which combines two kinds of treatments in one, is to attach a moxa cone to the top part of the needle that has already been inserted into the body. The moxa cone is then ignited and is allowed to burn to ashes. This method is quite widely used by both the Chinese and the Japanese.

Is Moxibustion Effective?

Like acupuncture, moxibustion has survived thousands of years. If it were not effective, it would not have lasted that long. The Chinese have used acupuncture and moxa therapy almost side by side since the beginning of acupuncture history. Thousands of years of clinical experiences have shown that often in a case where acupuncture treatment proves useless, moxibustion can yield good results quickly and easily. Based on the Yin-Yang theory and on the Eight Principles of diagnosis, an acupuncturist can easily determine from a patient's symptoms and appearance of the patient whether to use needle or moxa treatment. For patients who are diagnosed to have Yin pathogenic factors or cold syndromes, moxa can normally do a much better job than the needles can. However, if moxa treatment is improperly administered, it can easily lead to an adverse result, making the problem worse than before.

Since Ancient Moxibustion Was Sometimes Done With General Anesthesia or Localized Anesthesia, Which Involved No Pain And No Feeling, Is This Not in Direct Conflict With The Nerve Aspect Mentioned?

No. Ancient moxibustion treatment did not end when the moxa cone turned into ash. The direct scorching treatment method always resulted in a blister, which turned into a wound that required weeks to heal. Treatment took place when the body reacted to the wound until it was healed. If no wound occurred, the process had to be repeated until such time as a wound did occur.

CHAPTER FOUR
Diagnosis in Acupuncture

How Does An Acupuncturist Make A Diagnosis?

An acupuncturist makes a diagnosis by using the four diagnostic procedures developed a long time ago. These procedures have been used in traditional Chinese medicine and acupuncture ever since.

The four diagnostic procedures are: (1) observation, which includes the examination of the patient's face, eyes, the coating on the tongue, color and texture of the skin, posture, sensitivity, mood, and other appearances of the patient; (2) listening to patient's voice, breathing, and coughing, and noting odor from the mouth and other signs of sickness; (3) inquiry, which is probing and asking general questions related to the patient's complaint, appetite, taste, defecation, general health condition, and past medical history; (4) palpation or pulse taking, which is done by placing three fingers on patient's wrist in order to acquire clues for a diagnosis.

How is Pulse Taking Administered?

This is a very simple procedure done by placing three fingertips (the index finger, the middle finger, and the ring finger) on the radial arteries of the patient's wrists. Light, moderate, and deep touches are performed and the relative differences among the pulses provide clues for a diagnosis of the patient's physical conditions. On the whole, a strong pulse indicates an excess syndrome while a weak pulse indicates a deficiency syndrome, both of which reveal certain physical conditions. The light touches or deep touches by different fingers can also reveal some general conditions of the internal organs. Determining the quality of the pulse in terms of strength, frequency, and pattern requires very careful study and judgment, which are not easy to learn or master.

Who Formulated The Four Diagnostic Procedures?

The earliest documentation of the four diagnostic procedures is attributed to the legendary doctor Pien Chueh, who lived around the sixth century B.C. The historian Szuma Chien (who lived around 210 B.C.), who compiled *The Historical Records,* had several accounts of Pien Chueh, including Pien Chueh's use of the four diagnostic procedures. Szuma Chien was very impressed by Pien Chueh's outstanding skill in pulse diagnosis and went on to say that "as far as pulse taking is concerned, Pien Chueh is unparalled in the world." According to one study, Pien Chueh and his two apprentices were visiting Kao Kingdom (655 B.C.) when they heard that the prince had suddenly died. They hurried to the palace but by this time, the funeral preparations were actually under way. Pien Chueh examined the "dead prince," and a simple diagnostic procedure he used led him to believe that the dead prince was merely in a coma. He quickly instructed his apprentice Tzu Yang to administer acupuncture treatment, and after a little while, the supposedly "dead prince" woke up and surprised everybody. This incident made the legendary doctor even more legendary.

Is Pulse Taking As A Diagnostic Procedure Dependable?

Yes and no. Yes in the sense that it does reveal certain conditions of the body as a whole, and to some extent, conditions of certain organs. No because information acquired solely by pulse taking may not be sufficient and, therefore, may be undependable. Perhaps pulse taking is one of the many aspects of Chinese medicine that has led to a lot of bragging on the one hand, and to much controversy (especially among Westerners) on the other. It is not at all unusual to hear some Chinese patients say "I was amazed to discover that so and so took my pulse and immediately revealed to me that I have a kidney problem, which is right." A few acupuncturists even claim to be able to tell from pulse diagnosis how sexy a person is. A doctor of Chinese medicine or an acupuncturist, even blindfolded, is capable of acquiring some information about the general well-being of the patient and sometimes, about conditions of particular organs, by merely taking the pulse of the patient. However, an acupuncturist does not depend upon pulse taking as the only means of diagnosis. What he discovers from pulse taking is always considered together with the information he acquires from the other three diagnostic procedures mentioned above and with the Eight Principles related to the symptom complex.

Is Pulse Taking Easy To Learn?

No. Pulse taking is an art in itself. It is a unique aspect of Chinese intrinsic medicine considered by many to be recondite and elusive to grasp yet also fascinating to know. The art may take months to learn and years to master. Analysis and synthesis of pulse taking are so intertwined with the Yin and Yang theories that the technique appears like myth to Westerners at first glance. A few others may question its validity and even go so far as to say that it should be condemned. To the practitioners of traditional Chinese medicine or acupuncture, however, pulse taking is a diagnostic procedure that costs absolutely nothing, and it can yield instant information. To disregard it would be equivalent to throwing the baby out with the bath water.

Are The Four Diagnostic Procedures The Only Means An Acupuncturist Uses?

No. In the past decade or so, most of the practitioners of traditional Chinese medicine and acupuncturists have adopted from Western medicine a fifth diagnostic procedure, which is the laboratory testing method. In China, acupuncturists frequently order x-rays and other tests in addition to the four diagnostic procedures.

Besides of the five diagnostic procedures just mentioned, a knowledgeable acupuncturist has additional avenues for diagnosis, such as the ears and channel theories.

How Can The Ear Be Used For Diagnosis?

Over two thousand years ago, the Chinese had already discovered that meridians on the body were linked with the ear. *Neijing* states that the ear should not be considered as a separate organ because it is actually linked with all the internal organs of the body. Of the twelve meridians, all the six Yang meridians pass through the ear. The six Yin meridians also have links with the ear through the Yang meridians and the Extra meridians. The *Health Encyclopedia* (published in 1281 A.D.) of the Yung

Dynasty also concluded that the ear and the other organs of the body were inseparable.

Neijing also cited cases of kidney diagnosis through ear observation. The diagnostic observation is made possible by the natural tendency of the ear to reflect conditions of the internal organs: (a) by its shape, color, size, thickness, wrinkles, and the presence of blisters, hard knots, and so forth; (b) by its unusual sensitivity or pain to touch; and (c) by its sensitivity to electronic devices. These phenomena were discovered by the Chinese several hundred years ago, but on a small scale.

After 1950, extensive research on ear acupuncture undertaken by Dr. Paul Nogier of France greatly enriched knowledge of the relationship between the ear and the rest of the body. The new discoveries not only provided new convenient clues for diagnosis but also presented additional alternatives for treatment.

How Is Ear Diagnosis Done?

There are three ways in which ear diagnosis can be carried out:

(a) By observation with the naked eye. Unusual shape, color, scaly skin condition, blisters, hard knots, bone extention, and blood vessel conditions on the ear all indicate corresponding conditions of the internal organs or of other parts of the body.

(b) By the examination of sensitive spots on the ear with a probe (an object like a ball point pen). The exact location where sensitive spots occur reflects conditions of the corresponding internal organs and/or parts of the body.

(c) By the use of an electrical device. The device is capable of making discoveries beyond those possible with the naked eye and probe. The method is similar to (b) except that the probe is connected to an electrical device that sweeps the entire ear for low electrical resistance spots. When it hits low resistance spots, the device will give out signals with light or sound. The exact location of the spot on the ear provides clues for diagnosis.

How Can The Channel Theories Be Applied For Diagnosis?

The channel or the meridian theories in Chinese medicine govern not only acupuncture therapy but also physiology, pathology, and diagnosis. These theories are not new; in fact, they can be traced back all the way to *Neijing.* Diagnosis based on the channel theories depends upon information acquired from the pathological transmission of a symptom complex that corresponds to the channel theories. Diseases or ailments a patient suffers are often reflected along the meridians or on certain acupoints. These reflections occur in terms of unusual tenderness or pain to the touch. Until the last few decades, approximately twenty acupoints had been discovered to have diagnostic indications, and they were largely employed by old and well-experienced practitioners. The clinical applications of these acupoints for diagnosis were not very widespread, and what an individual practitioner could know was very limited in scope. But recently, the search for such diagnostic indications has mushroomed, and many practitioners and researchers have attempted to search for sensitive points all over the bodies of patients with confirmed diseases. Sporadic reports about findings have occurred in Chinese medical journals from time to time. By far the most extensive search for these acupoints was conducted by Gai Guocai and his fellow researchers of Peking. His 1982 second printing of *Diagnosis on*

Acupoints lists 140 kinds of ailments and health problems that can be diagnosed through acupoint examination.

What Are Some Examples?

— With lung disorders, for instance, there may be tenderness at the Zhongfu acupoint, or a nodule may be noticeable at the Feishu acupoint.

— With disorders of the liver, there may be tenderness at the Ganshu and Qimen acupoints.

— With the disorder of gastralgia, tenderness may be present at the Weishu and Zusanli acupoints.

For ten different kinds of cancer, Gai Guocai identified a common sensitive spot, the Sindaiqie acupoint (somewhere in the middle of upper leg hind side), that can be found on these patients. Some kind of tenderness will be felt when pressure is applied to the mentioned acupoint, and this indicates that there is a cancer in the patient's body. This sensitive spot is always accompanied by another sensitive acupoint along a certain meridian. Gai calls this second sensitive acupoint the "locating point" because it can indicate where the cancer is located.

CHAPTER FIVE
History of Acupuncture

How Old Is Acupuncture?

It is very difficult to determine exactly how long acupuncture has been in existence. The history of acupuncture reveals that the development of this art was very slow in its early stages. With this in mind, the following facts can offer some clues as to how old acupuncture is.

(1) The book *Neijing,* also known as the *Yellow Emperor Internal Medicine* (not by Yellow Emperor) was compiled during the Warring States (403-221 B.C.). This book contained all the fundamentals of acupuncture, including the major acupoints, theories of Yin-Yang and Five Elements, the twelve channels, principles of diagnosis, physiology, pathology, vital energy, concept of blood, and so on. *Neijing* offered the most conclusive information on acupuncture that was available at the time it was written. It is so advanced and outstanding that it has been considered the most authoritative reference on this subject even until the present era. Today, over two thousand years later, its content has seldom been challenged. Frequently, *Neijing* has been cited as a source of clues that led to many new discoveries. Practically speaking, this means that acupuncture as revealed by the book of *Neijing* had already reached an advanced stage over two thousands years ago. Before that stage could be reached,

many trials and errors and a great number of years must have transpired.

(2) Acupuncture is so old that it can be traced to the New Stone Age (8,000-2,000 B.C.) of the Chinese culture. This early dating was revealed by the stone acupuncture needles discovered in China. The evidence coincides with reports of ailments that were treated by bien (stone needles for acupuncture treatment). There are about one dozen books compiled around the 6th century B.C. that made reference to medical treatments by bien.

How Old Are The Oldest Acupuncture Needles Discovered in China?

(1) In 1963, an acupuncture needle made of stone was excavated in Mongolia. This needle, 4.5 centimeters in length and slightly flat with a pointed end, was identified by historians as dating back to the New Stone Age of the Chinese culture. This is the oldest acupuncture needle ever discovered.

(2) In 1978, an acupuncture needle made of copper, along with many other copper objects, was excavated in Mongolia. This is the oldest metal needle ever discovered and it has been identified as belonging to a period dating from the Warring States (403-221 B.C.) to Xi-Hang (206 B.C.-23 A.D.). It looks very much like a stone needle, which has led historians to believe that these copper needles could have come into use alongside the stone needles, before the stone needles were completely phased out.

(3) In Mancheng County of the Hebei Province, an ancient tomb of Liu Sheng (buried in 113 B.C.) was discovered and excavated in 1968. Among the relics found were nine acupuncture needles, four of which were made of gold and five of silver. The silver needles were

badly corroded, but the four golden ones were still in very good condition. These nine needles were of different lengths and shapes and could be identified with the nine kinds of acupuncture needles commonly used in ancient times.

How Could This Art That Was Practiced For So Long Remain Relatively Unknown To The World For Such A Long Time?

The answer is simple. The Chinese people were not explorers like the British, Spanish, or Portuguese. They remained aloof from the rest of the world until the 16th and 17th centuries, when Western countries discovered China and sent many missionaries there. Later, the requests by the West for trade relations were rejected by China repeatedly, until it was virtually at gunpoint that the door of China was finally opened for trade toward the end of the 19th century. It was only then that more of the Chinese culture was exposed to the West.

Did Acupuncture Enjoy Continual Acceptance In The Course Of Chinese History?

For acupuncture or any medicine to survive and flourish, it must have grass roots support. In a totalitarian country such as ancient China, endorsement by the government was important if not crucial. If the Emperor rejected a certain kind of medicine, then the only chance for that medicine to survive was for it to go underground, which made the whole situation more difficult. Thus, if any medicine was to survive and flourish in ancient China, nothing was better than for that medicine to perform a miracle for the Emperor's family.

As mentioned earlier, the *Historical Records* by Szuma Chien stated that the famous doctor Pien Chueh brought a dying prince who was in coma back to life. The fate of acupuncture was at that time solely in the hands of the Emperor, and nothing could have been a better recommendation for acupuncture than its use to save the life of a prince.

Hua Tao (110-207 A.D.) was considered one of the most famous if not the most famous doctor in ancient Chinese history. He was a good acupunturist as well as an outstanding surgeon. Hua Tao successfully treated with acupuncture the famous ruler Tsao Tsao, who suffered from prolonged headaches for which no treatment had proved helpful. Tsao Tsao even requested that Hua Tao become his personal physician, which Hua Tao repeatedly refused to do.

In 1034 A.D., Emperor Ren Zong of the Song Dynasty was paralyzed and received acupuncture treatments from Hsu Zi-yong, an acupuncturist of the Imperial Medical College. The Emperor recovered from his paralysis after just a few acupuncture treatments, and this amazed him so much that he inquired who the first person to discover acupuncture was. Hsu Zi-yong replied that it was Pien Chueh (which was not necessarily correct). The Emperor was so grateful to the discoverer that he ordered a temple to be built in Pien Chueh's honor.

Incidents such as these were of crucial importance to the survival of acupuncture in ancient times, and it was thus fortunate that they occurred from time to time.

Did The Ancient Chinese Government Support Acupuncture?

Yes. Throughout ancient Chinese history, governments of every dynasty stood behind acupuncture almost without exception. The government involvement in acupuncture started in the Sui Dynasty in 448 A.D., when the government took control of acupuncture and established a medical college to train acupuncturists and to provide acupuncture treatments. This governmental involvement was further expanded in 624 A.D. to create the Imperial Medical College during the Tang Dynasty. The college divided medicine into the branches of internal medicine, external medicine, pediatrics, and ear-eye-mouth-tooth. There were three major departments in the Imperial Medical College: the traditional Chinese medicine department, the acupuncture department, and the acupressure department. The medical college established at that time was so outstanding that it became the unchallenged model that safeguarded medical practice in China until the Qing Dynasty in the late nineteenth century. Not only did this college have a strong and lasting influence on Chinese medicine for a long time, but it was also quickly introduced to Japan and Korea.

Did The Imperial Medical College Make Any Contribution To the Advancement of Acupuncture?

Yes. Under Emperor Ren Zong's rule (1023-1063 A.D.), the need to preserve acupuncture knowledge was realized by Wang Weiyi, one of the chief doctors of the Imperial Medical College. The doctor appealed to the Emperor twice for permission to build a bronze acupuncture model but failed to get approval. Later, approval was granted when an indirect appeal was made through a member of the Emperor's family who was receiving treatments from the medical college. As a result, Wang Weiyi, who was an outstanding acupuncturist as well as an artist (stone carving), was entrusted with the responsibility of building the bronze model. Wang conducted a cross-section study of acupuncture literature and came out with a comprehensive version of *The Illustrated Manual on Acupoints for the Bronze Model* in 1026 A.D., and two life-size bronze acupuncture models in 1027 A.D. When the Emperor saw the models, he liked them so much that he ordered one to be kept in the palace and let the Imperial Medical College keep the other.

The significance and influence of the bronze models and of the *Illustrated Manual on Acupoints for the Bronze Model* far exceeded their original intention. They not only preserved acupuncture knowledge but also contributed to the unification of Chinese acupuncture nomenclature.

Can You Give A Little More Information About The Bronze Acupuncture Models?

The two bronze acupuncture models by Wang Weiyi were the first of their kind ever built in China, and of course their value to Chinese acupuncture was very great. The models were hollow inside, with holes made on all acupoints, and the names of meridians and acupoints were engraved on the outside of the models. The Imperial Medical College used one bronze model for teaching and test evaluation. In acupuncture examinations, the outside of the model was coated with bees wax and the inside of the model was filled with liquid. The bees wax covered the holes (acupoints) and also made them invisible. An accurate puncture on the acupoints allowed the needle to

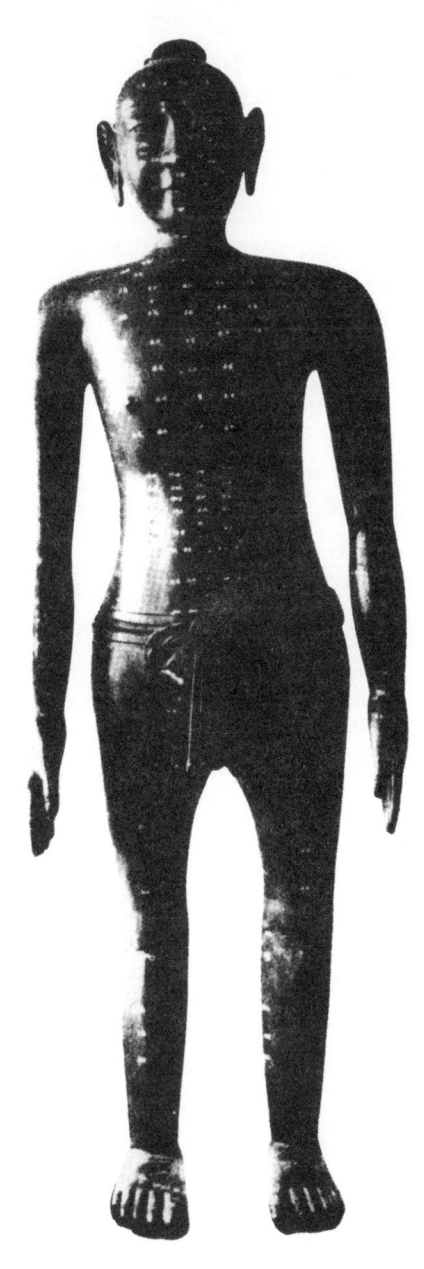

The bronze acupuncture model cast in 1443 A.D.

65

penetrate and caused the liquid to ooze out of the holes, while an inaccurate puncture hit nothing but the bronze.

During the Nansong Dynasty (1127-1279 A.D.), one of the bronze models was moved to Xiang Yang in the Hubei Province and was later lost. The other model was at one time seized by the Jin people but was later recaptured. After many years of service, the model was so worn out that repairs were carried out in 1265 A.D. and once again in 1443 A.D. Around the turn of the 19th century, the second bronze model by Wang Weiyi also disappeared from China. It is believed by some that this second one was taken by the Japanese during the war between the two countries and is now kept in Tokyo, Japan.

Were There Any Other Acupuncture Models Built After The First Two?

Yes. At the same time one of the existing models was being repaired in 1443 A.D. (during the Ming Dynasty), a new one was also built. Less than a hundred years later another attempt to reproduce the model was made under Emperor Jia Jing (1522-1566 A.D.). This time, Gao Wu, a doctor of the Imperial Medical College, built three bronze models—a man, woman, and child. The reproduction of bronze models in the Qing Dynasty under Emperor Qian Long (1737-1796 A.D.) was the last known attempt. Many bronze models were built during this time, and each foundryman who participated in the casting work was given one model. All in all, there were just over ten models built, but less than half a dozen are known to be still in existence. Apart from one kept in Tokyo, Japan (as mentioned earlier), Korea also possesses one (according to Chan-yuen Chen's *Topical Treatises,* published in 1983). All other remaining bronze models are dispersed in China.

Are There Any Significant Models That Were Built Recently?

Yes. In 1959, China produced the first life-size glass man showing not only the meridians and acupoints, but also the bones and internal organs. The model was built with individual light control for the 14 channels, internal organs, and all the major acupoints. A similar model has also been built by the Traditional Chinese Medicine Association in Hong Kong.

When Did Acupuncture Encounter Its First Major Setback In China?

Although acupuncture enjoyed popularity in China for thousands of years, it began to encounter difficulties at the end of the Qing Dynasty. This happened when the Emperor Dao Guang felt that it was an insult to his dignity to expose his body in order to receive acupuncture treatment. Thus, he issued an order in 1822 abolishing acupuncture from the Imperial Medical College and banning its use. All the government officials who had to please the Emperor tried to carry out effectively the order banning the use of acupuncture throughout the nation. This effort was so intense that in a short time, the use of acupuncture in public was quickly eradicated. However, the technique continued to be used underground, and it survived even in this difficult situation.

After the ban in 1822, acupuncture was not only confronting suppression from within, it was also encountering a new challenger from without—the arrival and practice of Western medicine.

Did The Guomindang Government Promote Acupuncture?

They did almost the reverse. After the Qing Dynasty was overrun by the Goumindang government in 1911, more and more hospitals and clinics practicing Western medicine mushroomed in China because the new government favored the new Western medicine instead of the Chinese intrinsic medicine (the traditional Chinese medicine and acupuncture). Wang Daixie, Minister of Education of the Bei-Yang government, began campaigning to abolish Chinese intrinsic medicine in 1912. Chan-yuen Chen of Hong Kong described in great detail (*Topical Treatises,* 1983) the attempts by a few Guomindang government officials then seeking to gradually abolish the Chinese intrinsic medicine. The boldest attempt was the bill (introduced by Yu Yan, a doctor of Western medicine) adopted by a special meeting of the Ministry of Health in 1929. The bill considered Chinese intrinsic medicine a stumbling block to other medical services and sought to set up six measures that included short-term plans and long-term plans to eventually phase out Chinese intrinsic medicine altogether. The six measures introduced sought to gradually restrict the practice of Chinese intrinsic medicine and ban the teaching and publishing of anything on that subject. The bill angered all practitioners of Chinese medicine and many other people as well. The attacks from numerous newspapers and many government officials, plus the general appeal made by the medical workers of Chinese intrinsic medicine to the Nanjing government on March 22-24, 1929, eventually forced the Health ministry to abrogate the bill.

The many years of campaigning by the few government officials to abolish Chinese intrinsic medicine not only failed, but the counter pressure it generated forced the government to give some legal status to the Chinese intrinsic medicine in 1931 and 1936.

There was an ironic episode in all this. Wang Jingwei, one of the highest government officials who had campaigned so openly and so diligently to abolish the Chinese medicine, was known to see a doctor of Chinese medicine when he himself was ill. Thus, Chinese medicine was something good for him but not good for his fellow countrymen.

What Has Been The Policy of the Chinese Communist Government Toward Acupuncture?

The Red Army adopted the traditional Chinese medicine, Western medicine, and acupuncture as early as the 1920s when they were engaged in hit-and-run wars with the Goumindang government. Since the communist government took over the mainland in 1949, they have been trying to give equal attention to all the three kinds of medicine they adopted. Furthermore, they have stood alone in the world in making the advancement of acupuncture a national priority. The government has not only taken the initiative in organizing acupuncture education and research, but it has also established thousands of acupuncture clinics throughout the nation to make acupuncture treatments available to everyone. Besides making acupuncture more popular and more readily available to all those who need it, many other significant accomplishments have also been made.

What Are Some Of These Significant Achievements In Acupuncture By The New Government?

(1) Publications. During the 38 years that the Guomindang government ruled the mainland, only three hundred papers on acupuncture and a few books were published. During the 35 years under the communist rule, some ten thousand papers and numerous other related works have been published, together with many ancient Chinese medical treatises that have been compiled, annotated, and revised. Many new medical journals are being added to the long list every year.

Until a few decades ago, Chinese acupuncture was mostly learned through apprenticeship. The overall competence of an acupuncturist varied significantly from acupuncturist to acupuncturist. It is true even to this day that many outstanding acupuncturists who are especially competent in handling certain kinds of problems will keep secret their special treatment techniques. The situation becomes unfortunate when these people die without passing on the secrets of these techniques. Because the communist state does not allow private enterprise, it has become less meaningful to keep secret these special techniques. Consequently, an unprecedented number of acupuncturists have made their special knowledge available to the public through journal publications. This is one of the main reasons why as many as ten thousand papers have been published in just 35 years.

(2) The integration of two schools of medicine. The integration of China's intrinsic medical technologies and Western medicine has been one of the major aims of the government of the People's Republic of China before it took power in China. The new policy marked the ren-

aissance of China's intrinsic medical technologies on the one hand, and the removal of the barriers and the rivalry between Chinese medicine and Western medicine on the other. The government has introduced traditional Chinese medicine and acupuncture into every hospital of Western medicine throughout the country, thus launching an integrated medical service for all patients. With this new setup in the hospitals and clinics, a number of diseases that might not be easily treated by just Western medicine, Chinese medicine, or acupuncture can now be handled by the integrated method.

The integration of the two schools of medicine is not being carried out only in the treatment room; it goes much further than that. Medical doctors from each of the schools of medicine are actually being encouraged to study the techniques, findings, and theories of their counterparts to ensure that the best treatment can be rendered to the patients. Some doctors of Western medicine who have participated in the integration method have said that the experience has enabled them to enjoy a new understanding of Chinese medicine and acupuncture. The old ill feeling and distrust toward the Chinese medicine and acupuncture have largely vanished.

The integration of the two schools of medicine has also enabled doctors of both schools to complement the weakness of one school with the strength of the other, thus resulting in a synthesized medical technology that incorporates the best features of both.

CHAPTER SIX
Dissemination

In The Past, How Was Acupuncture Taught In China?

There were four different ways:

(1) Through apprenticeship. Before the modern era, this method was by far the most popular one, and the greatest number of Chinese acupuncturists were educated in this way.

(2) Through apprenticeship within a family circle. Many expert Chinese acupuncturists would only impart the accumulated knowledge to their family members from generation to generation. This method produced the second largest number of acupuncturists in the past. A few outstanding books were also written by some unselfish acupuncturists who decided against the will of their ancestors to disclose generations of acupuncture knowledge to the public.

(3) Self teaching. Among the many outstanding Chinese acupuncturists, some had relied only on what they taught themselves to become competent and prominent.

(4) Institutionalized training. Institutionalized training started as early as 443 A.D. when the government of the Liu Song Dynasty of Nan Chao began to train acupuncturists.

Since then, the goverments of different dynasties always maintained a medical college for the training of acupuncturists. In the history of acupuncture, this method of teaching yielded poor results in training acupuncturists, both in terms of quality and quantity. However, in the past few decades, this method has become the dominant one as acupuncture training has shifted from private tutorship to institutions.

Besides China, Where Is Acupuncture Most Popular And How Did It Start There?

Besides China, acupuncture enjoys its greatest popularity in Japan, where it has a long history. Some Japanese acupuncturists claim that Chinese intrinsic medicine was introduced to Japan as early as 200 B.C., but the oldest written account may date it a bit later. The first account is that of Wang Ren, a Korean who brought acupuncture books from China to Japan in 340 A.D. Another account is that of a Chinese, Tze Chung, who brought Chinese acupuncture books to Japan in 562 A.D. However, neither account mentioned much that acupuncture was being learned and practiced by the Japanese. The literature that reached Japan might have generated enough curiosity so that in 608 A.D., two Japanese were sent to China to study acupuncture for fifteen years, after which they both returned to Japan to practice what they had learned.

The person who had the greatest influence in bringing acupuncture to Japan was a Chinese monk, Gian Chen, who was also a scholar and a doctor. The Japanese had known about him for years and had repeatedly (10 times) requested that he visit Japan. Monk Gian Chen tried five times in eleven years to cross the sea but each time was driven back by turbulent weather. He tried for the sixth time with twenty-three other monks and finally got to

Japan in the year 754 A.D. Gian Chen taught Buddhism and Chinese medicine in Japan until he died there ten years later. He was known to have cured the Japanese Empress from an illness and was remembered for his unselfish attempt to impart to the Japanese everything he knew about Chinese medicine. This man's contributions to and influences on both Buddhism and medicine at that time were so great that the Japanese erected a Buddha in his image after his death.

Shortly after the Imperial Medical College system was established (624 A.D.) in China, it was adopted by the Japanese. Since that time, Chinese medicine has enjoyed smooth development in Japan until the modern era. Today, Chinese intrinsic medicine is very deeply rooted in Japanese culture, and acupuncture is almost as popular in Japan as it is in China. There are forty-seven institutions in Japan exclusively established to teach and train acupuncturists. Next to China, Japan has the largest number of acupuncturists—about fifty thousand. There are also some twenty-seven acupuncture organizations that seek to promote acupuncture. In 1983, an acupuncture university was established in Japan, the first of its kind in the world. The institution offers a four-year training program leading to a bachelor's degree in acupuncture.

Is Chinese Medicine Also Popular In Japan?

The Japanese, as previously mentioned, have been involved in the use of Chinese intrinsic medicine for over a thousand years. Japanese usage of and accomplishments in Chinese intrinsic medicine are second only to those of China. It is obvious that the more the Japanese learn about the Chinese instrinsic medicine, the more involved they are in research and experiments with it.

In the past few decades, advancements in science and technology have enabled the Japanese to investigate Chinese intrinsic medicine using modern technologies. They have used computers and other electronic devices to analyze herbal medicine ingredients, and it seems that the better the tools they employ to investigate herbal medicines, the more amazing the discoveries they make. Over a thousand years of uninterrupted use of Chinese medicine and continuous investigations of such uses have led the Japanese to conclude that the advantages and the potentials of Oriental medicine deserve national attention. Thus, in 1982, the Japanese government decided to establish and fund "The Organization of Eastern Medicine Studies." Since then, diligent attempts have been under way to collect and analyze ancient Chinese medical works. Studies and research are also being conducted to use Chinese herbal medicine to combat 40 kinds of diseases for which Western medicine yields little or no answer. Currently, there are 150,000 Japanese doctors who practice Chinese medicine. This constitutes forty percent of all medical doctors in Japan.

While some Western people and even some Chinese themselves condemn Chinese medicine as "unscientific" or "superstitious," the Japanese hold quite a different view. Those who find acupuncture interesting should know that Chinese medicine has even more to offer.

How Was Acupuncture Introduced To Korea?

Since Korea is only separated from China by a river, Koreans had much less trouble learning Chinese acupuncture than did the Japanese. There are documented statements indicating that acupuncture was introduced to Korea in 541 A.D. Like Japan, Korea adopted the Chinese intrinsic medicine, and that, together with Korean herbal medicine, provided health care for the Koreans for over a thousand years before Western medicine was introduced there. As in Japan, Chinese medicine and acupuncture are still playing important roles in Korean health care to this day.

How Was Acupuncture Introduced To Europe?

Acupuncture was first introduced to Holland through literature by H. Busschof in the 17th century. Then in 1683, W.T. Rhyne introduced the practice to European countries. Some French hospitals attempted to use it but were not very successful.

In 1928, the French Ambassador, Soulie de Morant, brought Chinese medical books back to France and began a ceaseless effort to introduce acupuncture to the French people. Morant not only wrote extensively on the subject but also made a great effort to introduce acupuncture to hospitals and medical clinics. It was quite a long time before the French people realized the usefulness of acupuncture but once they started using it, its popularity slowly but steadily increased. In France today, acupuncture treatments are in most cases provided by hospitals.

After the French people started using acupuncture, literature on the subject became available. This French literature was then translated into some other European languages and thus contributed to the dissemination of acupuncture information to other European countries.

In 1950, the French physician, Dr. Paul Nogier, took a serious interest in the study of acupuncture and launched a major research on ear acupuncture, which he called "auricular medicine." Many years of continuous effort led Dr. Nogier to discover that human organs are reflected on the ear conch. This discovery is considered one of the very few significant contributions to acupuncture made by a non-Chinese. Because of Dr. Nogier's effort and influence, auricular medicine is becoming quite well known in European countries.

How Was Acupuncture Introduced To The West In Recent Times?

Just three to four decades ago, acupuncture was hardly mentioned in Western countries, but there are now a great number of people in the West who have heard about it. This rapid change has been brought about not by literature or by word of mouth, but mostly because of news media attention. It was the news media that effectively spread the word about acupuncture and made things happen.

By and large, acupuncture has been well presented in the Western news media, although unavoidably, there have sometimes been inaccurate or distorted views. In 1979, a radio station in a major city invited an acupuncturist to give an introductory talk on acupuncture to the audience in a talk show program. The acupuncturist traced the brief history of acupuncture and indicated that acupuncture was discovered and developed by the Chinese. He went on to say that in the modern era, the Chinese have been lagging behind in acupuncture research and it was a medical doctor in Vietnam who single-handledly advanced acupuncture to modern standards. But in fact, the acupuncture accomplishments in the modern era have been the results of thousands of acupuncturists and researchers. These accomplishments are well beyond what any individual could do in a lifetime.

In another instance, a well-known community figure made a trip to China in 1979 to investigate acupuncture. Upon returning, he reported to radio audiences that he had visited several acupuncture clinics in China and had observed acupuncture in clinical practices. He noted that the technique did indeed work. He even reported having seen a patient who came to a clinic limping and left walking normally. The careful investigation he conducted in China led him to conclude that "acupuncture is so much an integral part of the Chinese culture that it can be made to work by the Chinese for the Chinese. However, it is altogether a strange thing in the West, and it just won't work for the Westerners." Of course, investigations such as these are polemic at best.

Why Is It So Difficult For Acupuncture To Be Accepted In The West?

There are a few reasons:

(1) The Chinese people are by nature more practical than theoretical. They are so enculturated that questions of metaphysics seldom present a problem, and whether something is "scientific or not" is seldom a matter of concern. Perhaps it is just because the Chinese are more intuitive and subjective that they could accept acupuncture for thousands of years without inquiring how it works and whether it has a scientific basis.

People in the West are by nature more objective and more scientific. Subjective things are considered unreliable, and scientific scrutiny is the only vehicle through which anything can find justification for universal application. When Western medicine was first introduced into China in the late 19th century, the Chinese people never questioned this new knowledge and gladly accepted it. However, when the West was confronted with acupuncture from China, many felt that this new medical treatment method had to be subjected to more research, preferably at Western university research centers, before it could be accepted. Although the researchers who conduct experiments at these centers may be among the best- trained doctors in the world, few of them have the training and experience in acupuncture equal to their Chinese counterparts. The situation would lead one to conclude that the experimental results can be only as good as the acupuncture skills and knowledge of the researchers. Yet the West continues the redundant work, trying to discover again what the Chinese have already discovered, and the attempts go on and on.

(2) In nations where health care is good, there is less need for alternative medical care. In most cases, conventional health care management has been able to provide excellent medical services to people in the West. Thus, there is much less need for acupuncture in the West than there is elsewhere in the world, and this will continue to remain so.

(3) There may be some validity in the supposition that the policy of the West to maintain its doors shut or partially shut to acupuncture is due not to doubts about "whether acupuncture works," but rather to the fear that "it does."

(4) The relatively meager information available in the West on Chinese medicine constitutes a major problem with regard to its dissemination. While there are many Chinese who can read and speak Western languages, few Westerners have acquired sufficient language skills to speak or read Chinese. Furthermore, the ancient Chinese medical classics were written mostly in classic Chinese, which is so difficult that less than ten percent of very well educated Chinese dare to claim competency in it. Thus, unless some of the innumerable Chinese medical books and papers are translated into Western languages, they remain absolutely meaningless to the West. The lack of Chinese medical information available in the West naturally inhibits its assimilation by and dissemination to

Westerners. Furthermore, inaccurate information often compounds the problem and leads to misunderstanding. This is part of the reason why Chinese intrinsic medicine is sometimes labeled as "unscientific," "primitive," or "superstitious."

Since the World Health Organization (WHO) realized the feasibility of using acupuncture as an alternative means of medical management about ten years ago, it has been involved in the promotion and dissemination of acupuncture information to countries all over the world, and now acupuncture has spread to about one hundred countries in just a decade or so. However, after just a few study seminars held in China, the WHO experts quickly realized that there were "numerous obstacles" confronting dissemination. The major obstacle involves the fact that resources and research information on acupuncture are written mostly in Chinese, and no organized effort had ever been made to translate any of the much needed information to be shared with the rest of the world.

The World Health Organization is now trying to resolve some of these obstacles. They are seeking to establish an international nomenclature, a task which should have been undertaken many decades ago. Many Western countries have used different terminologies and numerical systems to translate Chinese acupuncture literature into their own languages. Because of this, acupuncture nomenclature in the West has been in a chaotic state that needlessly hampers transfer of knowledge. It is rather fortunate that the WHO experts had the insight to troubleshoot and to identify these major obstacles to dissemination. The decision by WHO experts to adopt the English numerical, the Chinese, and phonetic Chinese systems as the international acupuncture nomenclature will in the future make the transfer of acupuncture knowledge easier, and it will also afford easier access to the Chinese resources.

How Did Acupuncture
Come To The United States?

Although some books and periodical articles on acupuncture were in circulation in the United States prior to 1972, acupuncture remained by and large unknown to the American public until former President Nixon's visit to China, which stirred public attention about acupuncture, and thereafter, the demand for it.

Just like chiropractic, acupuncture also faced difficulties of acceptance at the beginning. Although some of the first acupuncture clinics in the country were closed by court order, the demand for this art has kept it alive for the past decade. To date, acupuncture has been legalized in more than ten states in the nation, although it still remains illegal in all other states.

In Countries Where Acupuncture Is Unknown,
How Would People Respond To It?

They would respond well if given the chance. The *Health News* of Peking, China, reported that a Chinese medical delegation made a friendship visit to Cairo, Egypt, in 1974. When it was revealed that there were few acupuncturists among the members of the delegation, the Egyptians made requests for treatments, and of course, the delegation was more than willing to demonstrate what acupuncture could do. Arrangements were then made for treatments to be rendered in a hospital in Cairo. After news of this spread, the response from the Egyptians was so enthusiastic that policemen had to be called in to keep order. As days went by, the crowd grew larger, and there were even patients flying in from nearby countries. The friendship visit, which had been intended to last only a few days, ended up lasting a few months, and the daily number of patients was still growing when the Chinese medical delegation left.

CHAPTER SEVEN
Acupuncture Anesthesia

When And How Was Acupuncture Anesthesia First Introduced?

Acupuncture anesthesia is the use of acupuncture treatment to eliminate a patient's pain while he remains fully conscious during surgery. This new method of anesthesia was discovered by the medical team of the No. 1 People's Hospital in Shanghai, China. The discovery was unintentional. After a tonsillectomy, a patient in the hospital was experiencing throat pain and could not swallow anything. The medical staff of the otolaryngology department attempted to remove the pain by an acupuncture treatment and achieved good results. Not only did the pain go away but the patient could also eat a bowl of meat dumplings immediately without a problem. This suggested to the medical staff that if acupuncture treatment could stop postoperation pain, it could also inhibit pain during the operation. The medical staff then began to conduct experiments on themselves (without actual incisions) to determine whether pain could be reduced or eliminated when an incision was made on the body. On August 31, 1958, the first operation to remove a tonsil tumor using acupuncture as the only means of anesthesia was performed. The patient experienced no pain throughout the operation, and this jubilant success was reported to many other hospitals. In the months that followed, the Liuchow Tuberculosis Hospital in Kwangsi and the No. 1 Tuberculosis Central Hospital in Shanghai immediately started to organize research groups to study and use acupuncture anesthesia for operations. A few months later, back operations and operations on the limbs, stomach, and chest were being carried out with acupuncture as the only means of anesthesia, and this new method worked remarkably well.

Did Acupuncture Anesthesia Gain Widespread Use In China Immediately After Its Introduction?

No. The widespread use of it has been quite slow. To improve the techniques and solve minor problems that occur in some operations using acupuncture anesthesia, a great deal of patience was necessary. The Chinese medical establishment did not act hastily. Whenever acupuncture anesthesia is used, sufficient research has been conducted to ensure the safety of the patient. Because of this careful approach, progress has been slow, but no life has been lost in surgery that can be attributed to acupuncture treatment. In the first eight years of using acupuncture anesthesia, only 10,000 surgeries were carried out using it. As techniques improved, it was used more frequently and for more kinds of operations. Its use spread from hospitals in the cities to smaller hospitals and clinics in the rural areas. Today, acupuncture anesthesia has been used more than 2½ million times. Satisfactory results have been achieved in some thirty kinds of operations, with the best results seen in operations on the head and neck.

Are The Acupoints Used For Anesthesia Altogether Different From Regular Acupoints?

Before I (THL) had acutally observed an operation using acupuncture anesthesia, I also wondered whether special points other than those regular acupoints were used. After having watched acupuncture anesthesia for the first time in Shanghai, I was surprised to see that the points used in that operation were no different from the points many acupuncturists used daily. I need to point out, however, that not all acupoints are good for anesthesia, and only certain points are good for inhibiting pain in particular areas and for purposes during an operation. There are also many new acupoints discovered that yield good results for anesthesia.

Where Are The Needles Inserted For Acupuncture Anesthesia?

During the early uses of acupuncture anesthesia, numerous needles were used and they were inserted all over the body. As the medical staffs reduced the number of needles used, they discovered from the Chingluo theory that many types of acupuncture anesthesia are possible and that they all yield good results. Thus, the original body needling for acupuncture anesthesia has now been expanded to ear-needling, foot-needling, face-needling, nose-needling, head-needling, ear-root-needling, and barefoot-doctor needling. Any of these needle treatments will be sufficient to inhibit pain during an operation.

How Many Needles Are Used
In Acupuncture Anesthesia?

Just like some acupuncturists who may start their acupuncture careers at first using many needles, the first acupuncture anesthesia performed in Shanghai, China, used a total of eighty needles. But shortly after the first attempt, the medical staff tried to simplify the process and reduce the number of needles being used. After over six hundred trials, they were positive that the number of needles could be greatly reduced. Thus, subsequent operations with acupuncture anesthesia were done with forty needles, then with twenty, then ten, and with fewer and fewer until medical staff were surprised that many operations could be carried out with only a few needles.

Today, most acupuncture anesthesia is conducted using about two pairs of needles, but when minor complications occur, more are added to control the situation. The Peking Tuberculosis Research Institute is known to have performed thousands of thoracic operations with just one needle, and the results have been very satisfactory and consistent.

Can Acupuncture Anesthesia Be Employed
For Open Heart Surgery?

Yes. In Western medicine, open heart surgery is more complicated than most other surgeries. Thus, acupuncture anesthesia use in open heart surgery also is more complicated. The first open heart surgery using acupuncture anesthesia did not come until April 19, 1972, over thirteen years after acupuncture anesthesia was first introduced and used.

The first use was on a 14-year-old girl for trilogy (pulmonary stenosis, atrial septal defect, and right ventricular hypertrophy). The patient went through the operation with a heart-lung machine hookup, was fully alert throughout the operation, and suffered no pain. She was able to eat on the same day she was operated on, and she could get out of bed on the fourth day after the operation.

Are There Any Advantages In Using Acupuncture Anesthesia Instead Of The Anesthestic Drug?

Yes. There is little doubt that drug anesthesia has a variety of side effects. For patients who have cardiac (heart), hepatic (liver), pulmonary (lung), or renal (kidney) problems, or for those who are physically very weak, drug anesthesia itself may create some risk to life, and sometimes these drug risks make it difficult for doctors to recommend surgery.

Acupuncture Anaesthesia, published by Foreign Language Press (Peking, 1972), reveals a very unusual case in China where acupuncture anesthesia truly gave hope to a patient. Shu-Hsuan Hu suffered from pyothorax, with pus and blood leaking from a fistula in his chest all year round. The patient was very weak, and many times the operations to remove pus resulted in heart failure and/or difficulty in breathing. When he became even weaker, it was apparent that he could not survive another general anesthesia. Unsuccessful operations, which were painful, were then done with local and spinal anesthesia. During his 24th and last operation, acupuncture anesthesia became available and was administered. What had not been done in all the previous operations was done during this operation. During the whole procedure, the patient was alert, calm, and in good spirits. His blood pressure and pulse remained steady. The surgical team not only was able to remove the pus as they had before, but they also were able to remove the fistula, close the cavity, and reset six ribs. The level of difficulty and the risk involved in this last operation were far greater than those of all previous operations. But this time, the patient was not near death as he had been many times before. The operation went smoothly, without any complication. Even more surprising was that the patient was able to cheer the surgical team during the operation. He could eat on the same day as the operation and he could get out of bed just three days later.

In another case of acupuncture anesthesia that may have saved a life, a woman in Alexandria, Egypt, had a caesarean section twice, and both times the babies were born dead because of the anesthetic drug. In her third pregnancy, the same method of delivery was used, but this time she had acupuncture anesthesia, and her baby was born alive.

What Are Some Of The Advantages Of Acupuncture Anesthesia?

Some of the most important advantages are:

— For those who have serious problems with high blood pressure, the liver, kidney, heart, or lungs, or for those who are physically very weak, this method offers operations with less risk.

— It is an alternative for patients who are allergic or oversensitive to anesthetic drugs.

— There are no side effects and fewer complications during and after the operation.

— Recuperation is much faster. Most patients can eat on the same day as the operation and can get out of bed in a few days. For minor surgeries, patients can resume eating and normal work soon after surgery.

— The patient's cooperation may be obtained during surgery. With facial, throat, or vocal cord surgery, this can greatly reduce nerve damage during surgery.

— Many kinds of operations using acupuncture anesthesia result in much less bleeding.

Are There Any Disadvantages To Acupuncture Anesthesia?

Yes there are, as it is not a method without shortcomings.

— After twenty-five years of research, experiments, and practical use, acupuncture anesthesia can be used effectively in only about thirty kinds of operations. The results for other operations have not been consistent, and the success rate has not been as high as is desired. For those operations in which acupuncture anesthesia does not yield consistent results, anesthetic drugs have to be administered in addition to the acupuncture anesthesia.

— In some patients, there is insufficient muscular relaxation, and some type of additional muscle relaxer has to be used.

— Surgery on internal organs with acupuncture treatment may confront organ contractions in some cases. This hinders the surgical process unless additional acupuncture treatment or drug supplements are administered.

— Some patients who are very timid will find it difficult to stay calm while the operation is under way.

— This method is still very much ignored and rejected by the West.

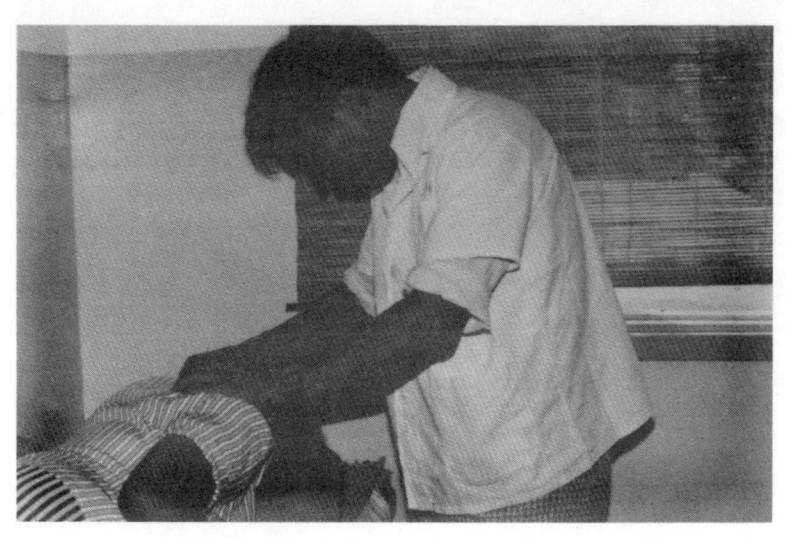

Author treating patients in China.

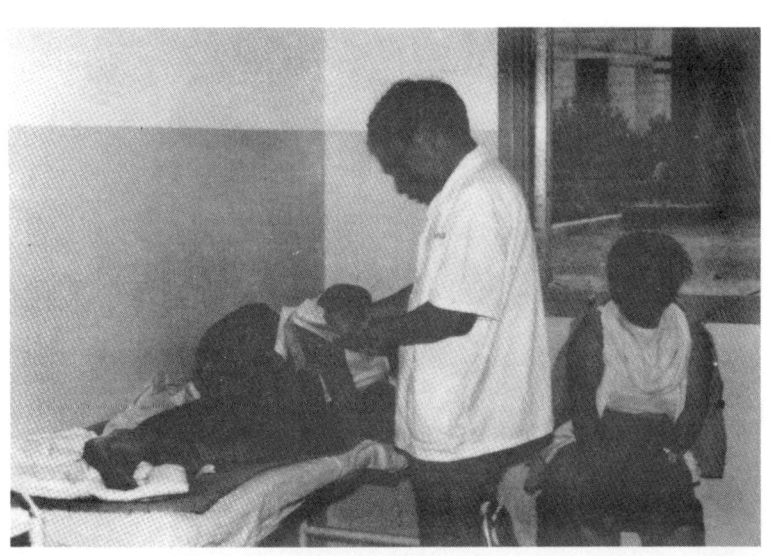

An acupuncture clinic waiting room (at a hospital) in China. This clinic sees about 500 patients daily.

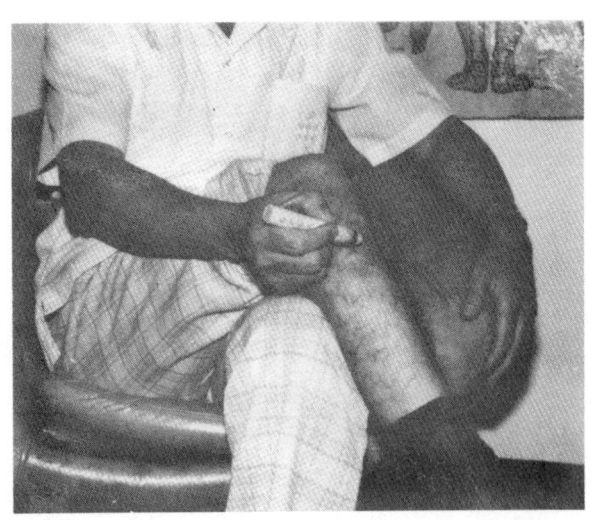

Moxa roll treatment on Zusanli acupoint.

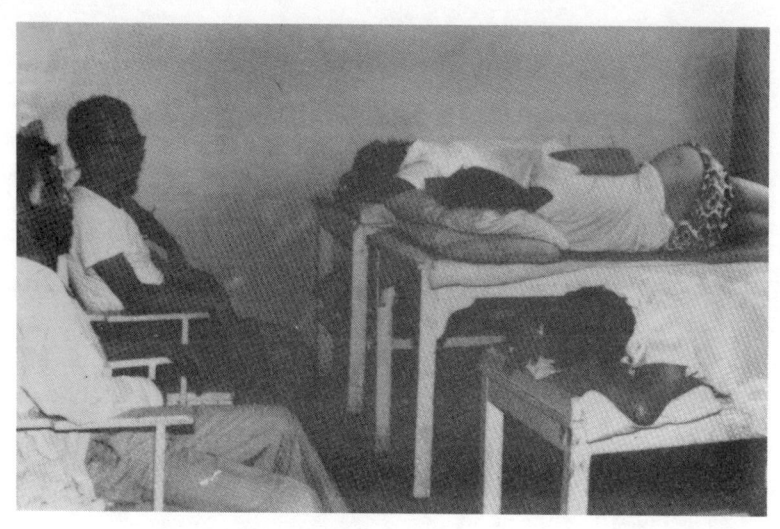

Acupuncture treatment rooms in China.

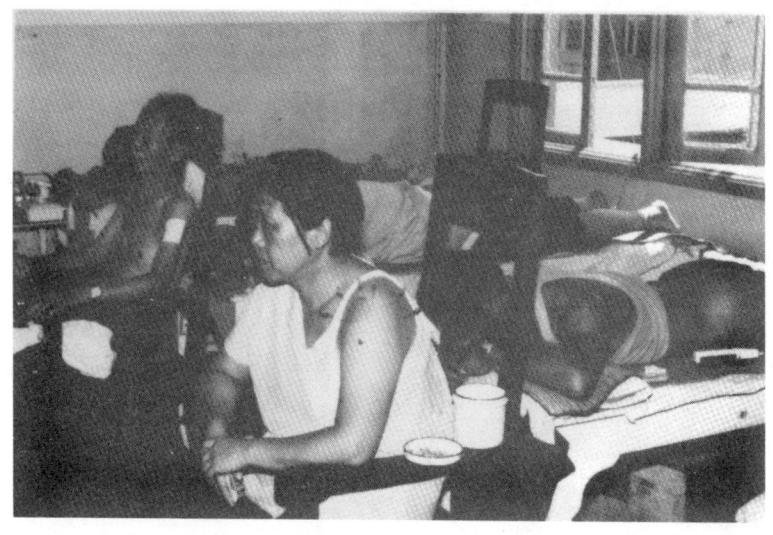

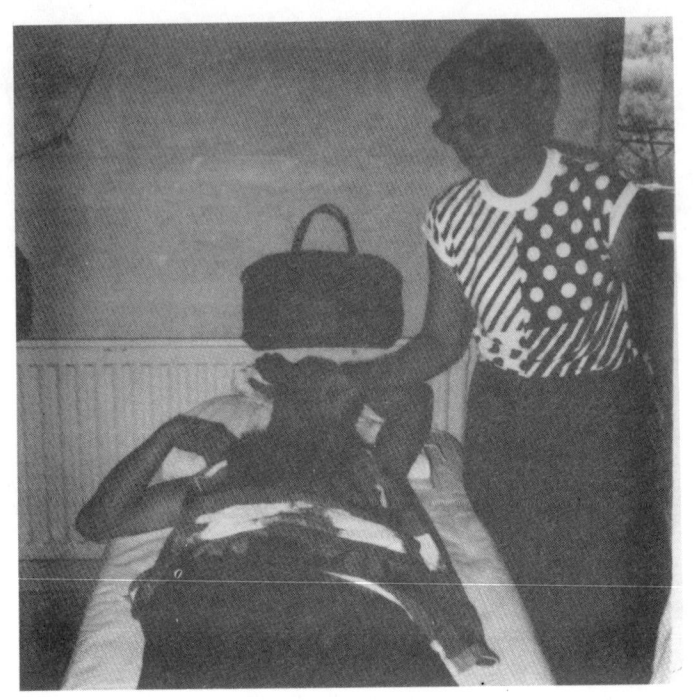

Moxa treatment administered in China with use of a device.

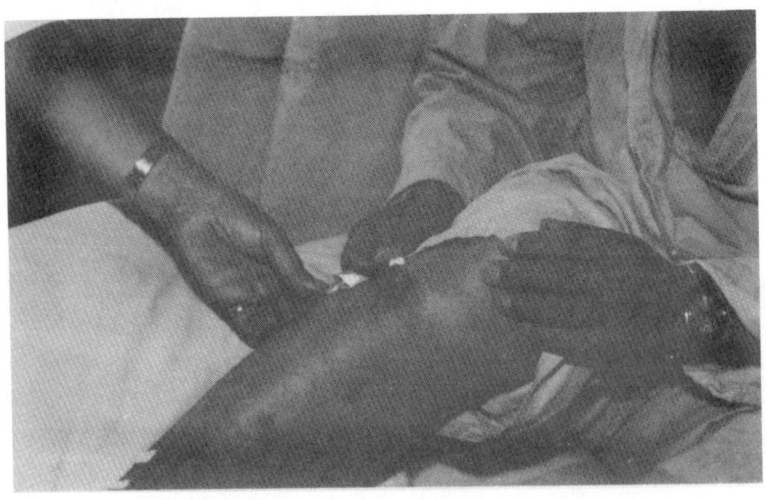

Moxisbustion administered in China. This picture shows the direct scorching or scarring method.

CHAPTER EIGHT
Clinical Potpourri

What Can Acupuncture Do?

The things acupuncture can do are just too numerous to list. The World Health Organization Inter-Regional Study Seminar recommended acupuncture treatment for about forty kinds of diseases, including neural, muscular, and gastrointestinal disorders, and disorders of the mouth, eye, and respiratory system. The *Jao Guorui's Cumulative Clinical Experiences on Acupuncture,* published in China in 1979, lists three hundred kinds of diseases and medical problems that can be treated by acupuncture with different levels of success.

Is Acupuncture Treatment Good For Any Kind Of Disease?

No. There are many kinds of diseases for which acupuncture is ineffective.

How Is The Acupuncture Needle Inserted?

There are numerous ways to insert a needle. Two of the most popular ones are mentioned here.

(a) By using finger manipulation. The needle is held with the thumb and index figure or with the thumb, index, and middle fingers positioned relatively close to the tip, with or without help from the fingers of the other hand. The needle is then inserted under the skin with a quick motion. The quick motion is to reduce the duration of pain because the skin is most sensitive and the greatest pain is experienced when the needle first touches the skin. After the needle gets under the skin, the slower movement is used to achieve deeper penetration. In most circumstances, much less pain is experienced from the second part of the procedure, when deeper penetration is achieved.

(b) By using a guide tube. This method uses smaller needles, which may cause slightly less pain. The guide tube is first placed on the acupoint with the needle inside the tube. Then with a gentle but forceful tap on the top end of the needle, it goes through the skin. The guide tube is then removed and the slower movement follows to achieve deeper penetration, just as described in the first method.

Is The Guide Tube Method Better?

Not necessarily. It is much harder to learn to insert the needle with finger manipulation. However, if one has mastered the skill, he may be able to do it with as little pain as from the guide tube method. The Chinese usually prefer to use finger manipulation. The guide tube method is easier to learn and slightly more cumbersome to use. The Japanese prefer this method, and it is the predominant method used by them and by acupuncturists in the West who have been influenced by them.

How Many Needles Are Usually Used For A Treatment?

A competent acupuncturist uses about three pairs of needles for the treatment of one ailment. Sometimes, there can be a few more or less depending on the ailment. Many ailments can actually be treated with just two needles, but others may require as many as six or more, but seldom more than ten. If a patient has more than one ailment, then more needles will naturally be required.

Is It Better To Have More Needles Used Or Less Needles Used?

If it is a matter of preference, then you need to know a little bit more to make a better decision. We read a published article on the introduction of acupuncture in which the writer mentioned that for an ordinary treatment, "hundreds of needles were used." That is unnecessary. Of course, the writer knew very little about acupuncture and certainly did not know that a patient does not have to be a pin cushion to receive an effective acupuncture treatment. Most Western people are more familiar with acupuncture treatments that call for the use of many needles. Possibly, those who were first exposed to acupuncture were treated by acupuncturists who had to use a lot of needles to ensure some results and, because of this, it was thought that acupuncture treatment unavoidably involves many needles. A sharpshooter can kill a bird in the tree with a rifle while another one may need to use a shotgun to ensure any chance at all.

Another article in a Chinese paper some years ago told of an old Chinese acupuncturist who was trying to tell his friends in China about his practice in the West. He mentioned that acupuncture patients in the West thought that more needles might produce better results. Thus, although this acupuncturist had been trained to use just a few needles in a treatment, he ended up using a large number of needles for every patient who had such a preference. He felt sorry about making them pin cushions, but he could not afford not to please his patients. Actually, acupuncture treatment using many needles is not necessarily a bargain.

Is The Use Of Fewer Points Or Fewer Needles Considered An Improved Method Or A More Modern Technique?

Actually, the possibility of treating an ailment with very few needles or even with one needle is not at all new. Hua Tao (141-208 A.D.), one of the most famous medical doctors in Chinese history, was known not only as the first surgeon to use his own general anesthesia drug "mafusan," but he was also known as an outstanding acupuncturist who usually used just one or two needles in treatment and got very good results. The *Biography of Hua Tao,* compiled by historian Fan Yeh (398-446 A.D.), related that Tsao Tsao (155-220 A.D.), a very well known statesman, strategist, and poet, often had headaches and had tried all means of treatment without any results. Eventually, it was Hua Tao who removed Tsao Tsao's headache using acupuncture with just one needle. The Chinese like to describe a very competent acupuncturist as one who can produce results with just one needle. Thus, to some extent it is true that even if a person does not know much about acupuncture, he can tell how competent an acupuncturist is by the number of needles needed to produce good results.

Is Any Kind Of Drug Applied On The Needles?

This question is asked very frequently, and the answer is "absolutely no." All acupuncture needles are sterilized prior to being used. Just before needle insertion, the needles are again cleansed with a cotton ball soaked in alcohol. There is absolutely no magic drug or any kind of solution used on the needles in acupuncture treatments.

Can Acupuncture Patients Get Different Results From Different Acupuncturists?

Yes. Good acupuncture treatment depends on (1) correct diagnosis, (2) good acupoint prescription, (3) skillfulness in needle insertion and manipulation, and (4) resourcefulness of the acupuncturist in improvising backup treatments if one attempt fails. All these factors can determine the outcome of the treatments. Furthermore, it is not unusual for a patient to get good results from one acupuncturist with but a single treatment, whereas it may take two or three treatments to get the same results from another acupuncturist.

Will Different Acupuncturists Achieve Different Results Even Though They Use The Same Acupoints Prescribed To Treat A Given Ailment?

Sometimes they will. This is because inserting a needle in the right place does not necessarily guarantee good results. There are two factors that can play a vital role in treatment outcome.

(1) To achieve good results, the needle has to be inserted and manipulated to the point at which "Qi" is attained. When this happens, the patient may feel

numbness, swelling, soreness, or distension around where the needle is inserted. One woman who had severe sinus problems was treated by an acupuncturist more than ten times. Each time, the treatment helped for a few days, but then the problem came back. She then went to another acupuncturist who asked where her previous acupuncturist had inserted the needles when treating her. The acupoints that the previous acupuncturist had used were the best known ones. The problem was not poor acupoint prescription, but it could have been poor response on the part of the patient or the lack of treatment skills by the previous acupuncturist. When receiving her first treatment under this second acupuncturist, the patient said that she had never felt this good in all her previous treatments. After just two treatments by the second acupuncturist, her problem went away.

(2) According to the Yin-Yang theory, most diseases carry either Xu (deficiency nature or underactivity) or Shi (excess nature or overactivity). This determines whether Bu (reinforcing or tonification) or Xie (reducing or sedation) should be followed in needle manipulations. This important aspect of needle manipulation is often difficult to grasp or even intentionally ignored by those who have less respect for the Yin-Yang theory and Eight Principles.

Do All Acupuncturists Prescribe The Same Acupoints For A Given Disease?

No. Unlike Western medicine, acupuncture therapy is not very standardized as yet. Anyone who has read a few dozen acupuncture books will probably find that the Chinese have tried to use acupuncture treatment for just about every kind of disease or ailment known and that for each disease or ailment, numerous acupoints have been recommended. There is now enough evidence to conclude that acupuncture can truly be used to treat many diseases and ailments, but is by no means a cure for all illnesses. As for all the acupoints that have been recommended to treat numerous diseases or ailments, some work very well, some yield fair results, and some may not work at all. Thus, if a person has arthritis of the hand and consults half a dozen acupuncture books to look for acupoint prescriptions, he will most likely find that each book recomments different combinations of acupoints, and that some points may be the same but most of them will be different. Furthermore, these different acupoint recommendations may yield the same clinical results or they may yield different results.

Twice in my acupuncture practice, I (THL) have learned very effective but otherwise unusual acupuncture treatment techniques from somebody who knew almost nothing about acupuncture aside from having been treated by acupuncturists. On both occasions, the patients told me what diseases they suffered from and what the acupuncturists did to resolve their problems. What surprised me was not the treatment results, but rather the very unusual acupoint prescriptions, which are not found in any book or journal known to me. I used the same point prescriptions in my practice and found they do yield good results.

So quite obviously, if half a dozen acupuncturists are asked to treat the same patient for a given disease, the chances that they will all give identical acupoint prescriptions are almost nil unless they all studied under the same teacher and never learned anything beyond that. If the six acupuncturists are from different educational backgrounds, the points they recommend could have some similarity or they could be altogether different, depending on the ailment being treated.

Is There An Acupuncturist Who Is Capable Of Listing All The Best Acupoint Prescriptions For All the Known Treatable Ailments?

This would be desirable, but it is still quite impossible for anyone to do now. Many acupuncture treatment secrets have yet to be disclosed, verified, and tested on a large scale in a clinical setting so that more dependable and scientific conclusions can be drawn. This is something in which the Chinese medical workers are far behind their Western counterparts. But it is not without reason.

What Are The Reasons?

Confucius says, "those who know speak not, those who speak know not." While this may not be characteristic of all Chinese, it does correctly depict some. Whether it is from Confucius' teachings or from that of other sages, some Chinese of exceptional caliber have the peculiar tendency to shun public recognition and avoid the celebrity image. Instead of accepting public praise and admiration gracefully, they react with humble denial. It is customary for most educated Chinese to react to praise by saying "qi gan, qi gan," which literally means "how dare, how dare," implying "how dare I claim to be worthy of such recognition." Most likely, he will then immediately divert attention to something else. There are always some acupuncturists of exceptional caliber who have the most to contribute, yet say the least and prefer to live in oblivion.

When we were visiting acupuncture clinics in China, we discovered unfamiliar acupoint selections or treatment techniques used in almost one of every three clinics we visited. They are unfamiliar in the sense that they are seldom or never mentioned in acupuncture literature that we know of. Thus, there is still a lot of valuable knowledge that has not yet found its way into the acupuncture literature.

Because of this, Hao Jin-kai of China spent thirty years searching and collecting effective acupoints and acupoint prescriptions that had not been disclosed in China. The two volumes of *Extra Acupoints,* published in 1963 and 1973, respectively, are outstanding accomplishments even though no scrutiny was undertaken.

Do The Chinese Keep Trade Secrets?

The keeping of trade secrets is of course nothing new. It is done by people everywhere in the world and the Chinese are no exception. Because of the absence of patent law and copyright law, the Chinese have done it well in the past. When they discovered special medical treatment methods or techniques, they always kept them secret and passed them down only within their family circle from generation to generation. There were two general guidelines used to protect the secrets. First, the secrets were to be "revealed only to the insiders but never to outsiders." This means that the secrets were told only to somebody within the family circle. The second guideline was "reveal to your sons but not to your daughters." Chinese society is a male-dominated one. When a girl marries, she then belongs to another clan, and this excludes her from her parents' family circle. Thus, no secret should be revealed to women in order to prevent future disclosure of the secret to the family into which the daughters will marry. In our family, if we have a secret and have to abide by the guidelines, we will have a real problem because all our children are girls!

Although there is much less of a tendency to keep medical secrets now than there was many years ago, it is still being done, particularly by Chinese in the free world, where competition for business exists. Sometimes an expert Chinese acupuncturist may teach or write, but he may still keep some of the very best information to himself in order to retain supremacy.

Do Most Of The Achievements In Acupuncture Or Chinese Medicine Come Easily?

Not at all. As was mentioned earlier, the examination of acupoints as a method of diagnosis has been the work of scores of acupuncturists. It took over twenty years of continuous search in theories and in clinical settings before something more conclusive could be drawn, and the work is still far from complete.

In Chinese medical history, seldom have great discoveries been made as a result of intelligence alone. The contributors were mostly common people whose endless efforts made things happen. One such person was an oncologist in China whose story appeared in the *International News* just recently. Some 20 years ago, Miss Wang Shu-hua at the age of twenty was found to have adrenal gland cancer. She was very scared but not completely without hope. Her grandfather, a doctor of Chinese medicine, was particularly known for his special herb that could cure some kinds of cancer. Because of numerous tumors (some as big as dumplings) that he had cured, he had the nickname "Big Dumpling Wang." However, the grandfather did not pass the secret of his special herb on to any other doctor or to anyone in his family before he died. Wang Shu-hua's mother remembered roughly where the grandfather had gone to collect the herb, and there were still two bags of it left when he died. Three months after Wang Shu-hua took the herb, her blood pressure was down and her cancer was cured.

But the herb had run out. Of course, the young girl experienced a terrible sense of loss and she was determined to identify the herb. Since she could distinguish the taste of it and she knew roughly where it was collected, although the exact location was not known, she began searching over the mountain where the grandfather had gone to collect the herb. She tasted one herb every two hours and examined about four to five herbs daily. During the search, she was seriously poisoned four times. On one occasion, she tasted one plant that caused her to lose her mind for a day, with uncontrolled shouting, crying, and laughing. On another occasion, she tried another poisonous plant that caused kidney failure and a swollen body due to water retention. However, she was so determined to identify the herb that almost no hardship or danger could stop her. After two and a half months of intensive searching, the effort paid off with her 149th try. She found the right plant in a valley where snakes like to gather.

The success she had with the herb led her in 1969 to a job in a local hospital where she used the herb to treat cancer patients and at the same time did cancer research. Not long afterwards, her contributions to cancer control led her to a promotion which made her oncologist at a hospital in Ge Nang. In 1982, another promotion brought her to one of the most outstanding hospitals of Chinese medicine in the nation, the Kwanganmeng Hospital in Peking.

Her efforts in medicine have saved thousands of lives (patients with certain early-stage cancers), including those of a few government officials of the highest ranking. Unlike her grandfather, who one may consider "inscrutable," Dr. Wang Shu-hua is compiling a book on her discoveries.

Is There Any Place On The Body Where An Acupuncture Needle Should Not Be Inserted?

It is understandable that no needle should be inserted directly on any vital organs of the body. Apart from these places, ancient acupuncture classics have been careful to list some two dozen acupoints as off-limits to needle treatment, and some fifty acupoints on which no moxibustion should be administered. During the past 30 years, numerous experiments have directly or indirectly challenged these restrictions and now, fewer restrictions on these points are being observed. The restrictions were imposed by the ancient literature because of the sizes of the ancient needles, some of which were ten times larger than those used today. Larger needles could cause some problems in the restricted areas. Moreover, the lack of anatomical knowledge in ancient times was another reason why the restrictions were set well beyond the safety limits.

When Is It Best To Have Acupuncture Treatment?

If the treatment is for pain, it is advantageous for the patient to come to an acupuncture clinic when he has the pain. The reasons are as follows:

(1) For most pain problems treatable by acupuncture, immediate results can be expected. Thus, if a patient comes in with pain and leaves without it, he or she will know right away whether there has been a response to treatment.

(2) If the patient comes in with the problem, the acupuncturist will have more information to work with. If the first point prescription does not work, a second attempt can be made.

Should A Patient Observe Any Restrictions After An Acupuncture Treatment?

With treatments for a backache or pain in a large joint, it is advisable for the patient not to engage in excessive exercise or movement right after the treatment. Such restriction should be observed for a few days. A sudden removal of pain followed by excessive exercise may lead to even more pain for awhile.

Is There Any Pain Involved When An Acupuncture Needle Is Being Inserted?

It is sometimes true that certain acupoints on the body are less sensitive than others, and the insertion of needles at these points involves very little pain or at times, no pain. But to say that the insertion of a needle into the body involves no pain at all, as some may claim, is usually not true. Virtually any needle inserted into the body will be felt, and a minimum level of pain will be experienced. On the whole, the pain that a patient experiences in an acupuncture treatment is generally much less than what is feared or expected. In addition, different persons have different levels of tolerance for pain as well as different levels of sensitivity to pain. Even the same person may feel more (or less) pain at different times.

Can The Level Of Pain Experienced From Needle Insertion Be Different With Different Acupuncturists?

There may be a slight difference. A very experienced acupuncturist can insert a needle with little pain while the same needle in the hands of someone else can cause a bit more pain. How the needles are inserted and the skill of the acupuncturist can make a little difference.

Can An Acupuncture Needle Break Inside The Body?

For thousands of years, the breaking of needles inside the body and their subsequent removal were major concerns in acupuncture treatments even though in most cases, the incident did not constitute a life-threatening danger. The invention of stainless steel has eliminated most if not all the worry about broken needles. It is actually quite difficult to break a stainless steel acupuncture needle without the use of a cutter. Thus, with the stainless steel needles now employed, it is most unlikely that they will break under normal use.

Can One Take Acupuncture Treatment At Any Time?

Yes, but there are some situations in which an acupuncture treatment should not be given or should be given only with great care. They are:

(1) For patients with heart problems who are physically very weak, it is better not to give a treatment or to give it with extreme care.

(2) For pregnant women, the same precautions apply.

(3) On acupuncture points where scars or warts exist.

(4) With any patients who are physically weak, great precaution should be taken.

(5) For patients who wear heart pacers, no electric stimulator should be applied.

(6) When a patient is too hungry, tired, or drunk.

(7) If there are other unusual physical conditions.

Is Acupuncture Treatment Dangerous?

Acupuncture treatment is relatively safe. In thousands of years of practice and countless treatments, there have been accidents, but extremely few considering the great number of treatments that have been administered. Those accidents that did occur happened mostly in China and were related to carelessness and ignorance. Just as a knife and a pair of scissors in the hands of a surgeon can help but also hurt if incorrectly used, so can acupuncture needles in the hands of an acupuncturist help but also hurt if incorrectly used.

Can Some Minor Accidents Occur Under Acupuncture Treatment?

Yes, but very rarely. There have been reports from China that needles inserted on the Neiguan, Huantiao, Tientu, and Weichung points may result in some very minor tingling or pain problems but this occurs so rarely that it is almost not worth mentioning. If it does occur, a knowledgeable acupuncturist can always insert a few needles to correct the problem instantly since most of the solutions for these problems have already been discovered. I (THL) once treated a patient for nervousness. The desired result was achieved, but the patient traded nervousness for tingling in one of the fingers. When the patient came back on the fifth day with a tingling finger, I barely touched an acupoint and the tingling feeling went away instantly. Without the treatment, the tingling might have lasted for some days, but it would eventually have gone away by itself.

Does Acupuncture Treatment Work
For Everyone Every Time?

No. On the whole, the chances of responding to acupuncture treatment vary from person to person and from case to case. For an ailment that is treatable by acupuncture, the likelihood of achieving a response generally ranges from 75% to over 90% depending on the kind of ailment. There is always a small percentage of patients who will not respond to treatment. However, even if a patient does not respond to treatment for one ailment, he or she may respond very well to treatment for another ailment. Thus, if Mr. A. does not respond to treatment for sciatica, he still may respond very well to treatment for headache or sinus problems. A situation in which a person failed to respond to acupuncture treatment for any ailment he suffered has never been identified.

Why Do Some People Sometimes Not Respond
To Acupuncture Treatment or Respond Poorly?

There can be many reasons:

(1) For unknown reasons.

(2) It may be poor acupoint selection or even use of the wrong points.

(3) Incidents of poor response or nonresponse can occur when acupuncture needles are inserted on spots of the patient's body where sensitivity is very poor or paralyzed.

(4) As mentioned earlier, the nature of diseases can carry Xu (deficiency syndromes or underactivity) or Shi (excess syndromes or overactivity). Needle manipulation can only be either Bu (reinforcing or tonification) or Xie (reducing or sedation), and Bu

manipulation must be used for diseases with Xu syndromes, while Xie manipulation must be used for diseases with Shi syndromes. The incorrect needle manipulation will at times lead to poor results or to no results at all, even though the acupoints are very well selected and all needles are inserted right on the acupoints.

(5) In a research paper reported at the Second National Acupuncture Symposium, held in Peking in 1984, Dr. Tang Dean of Tianjin, China, revealed that female patients with elevated serum estradiol levels generally showed better treatment results and that patients with Yang Xu (Yang deficiency) generally responded better than did those with Yin Xu (Yin deficiency).

(6) Insufficient numbers of treatments. Some diseases of a chronic nature may need many treatments before results can be forthcoming.

(7) Insufficient treatment time. This is seldom a problem.

(8) Wrong diagnosis.

Some People Will Faint While Receiving An Injection Or While Donating Blood. Can This Happen To These Same People While They Are Receiving Acupuncture Treatment?

Most likely. Although it is very rare, there are always some people who cannot tolerate needles in their bodies. With these people, dizziness may occur after an injection or when acupuncture needles are inserted in the body.

Is There Any Danger If This Happens?

No. If this happens, the needles should be carefully withdrawn and the patient should be helped to lay down to rest. The patient will recover after a few minutes.

Since More Women Than Men Are Afraid Of Needles, Are Women More Apt To Feel Dizzy?

No. In fact, the reverse is true. This happens more frequently to men than to women. Sometimes a man who looks strong and robust may not be able to take a tiny needle. In any case, the likelihood of a patient's feeling dizzy after a needle is inserted is very slim indeed. There are even some people who may pass out after just seeing blood or seeing a needle being inserted into someone else's body, but the chances of encountering such a person are even more rare.

Are There Some Acupoints That Tend To Cause Dizziness More Than Others?

Yes. There are some points on the limbs, head, and back that can cause dizziness in a very few patients when they receive treatment while seated. The problem may not occur if the patient receives the treatment lying on a bed. A very few acupoints are known to cause dizziness in a few patients even when they receive treatment lying down. These patients should consider moxibustion if it is feasible, and possibly should not have acupuncture at all.

Why Should A Person Not Take An Acupuncture Treatment If He Or She Is Too Hungry Or Too Full?

It is easier for a person to feel dizzy if he or she is either too hungry or too full while receiving an acupuncture treatment. When I (THL) was learning acupuncture in Shanghai, a teacher told us an interesting story about his trip to an African nation. As a clinical expert, he was stunned by what happened at the first treatment session, held in the afternoon shortly after his arrival in that country. What surprised him was that patient after patient passed out and had to lie down on the floor. After a while, the floor became crowded, and the doctor just could not figure out what had gone wrong. Later, after extensive questioning, he found out that these patients were all Muslims, and their treatments had been given late in the afternoon in the month of Ramadan, when the Muslims fast.

Can More Than One Ailment Be Treated At The Same Time?

Yes. There is almost no limit to the number of ailments that can be treated at a given time. For example, a person can have headache, sinus, arthritis, indigestion, and knee problems all treated at the same time. There is no evidence that any undesirable effects can result from multiple treatments. Since it saves both time and money, why not have multiple treatments rather than treat one ailment at a time?

What Treatment Intervals Are Most Realistic And Economical?

The name of the game is to achieve the most benefit with the least number of treatments. We have known acupuncturists who require patients to take treatments every other day for a few weeks. Of course, there is no harm in having one or even two treatments daily, but this will be more expensive for the patient. As a general guideline, an interval between treatments of about four days is typical and essential. For patients with paralysis and some chronic problems, slightly more frequent treatments may be more desirable or even necessary. Whatever the number of treatments or their frequency, it is always smart to continue treatment as long as progress is being made and to discontinue treatment or look for another acupuncturist if no results are in sight after a few sessions.

How Deep Are The Acupuncture Needles Inserted?

It depends on three factors:

(a) Where the needles are being inserted. If a needle is being inserted into the hip to treat sciatic nerve pain, the insertion can be quite deep. If a needle is being inserted into the limbs, the insertion can be an inch or so in depth. If the needle is being inserted into the ear, then the insertion is very shallow—just enough for the needle to hang onto the ear.

(b) The size of the patient. If the needles are to be inserted into the body or the limbs of someone who is large and heavy, then the insertion may be slightly deeper than it would be for someone who is very small or skinny.

116

(c) How or in what positions a needle is being inserted. The transversal insertion may call for a little deeper insertion.

How Soon After An Acupuncture Treatment Can One Expect Results?

It varies. For most pain problems, results are usually immediate. That is to say, a person may come to an acupuncture clinic with pain and he or she may be able to leave with less pain or no pain at all. However, with some chronic problems, quite a few treatments may be required in order to see some results.

Can Acupuncture Treatment Be Used For Birth Control?

No. If it could, it would be very good news for China, where overpopulation has been a problem. After many years of research, the Tsimen acupoint was thought of as being good for birth control if rendered to women. From 1958 to 1960, several hospitals in Shanghai carried out clinical experiments to determine whether acupuncture treatment alone could prevent pregnancy. The results were rather disappointing. The same experiments were also carried out in Canton and in some other cities, and nowhere were satsifactory results reported. Thereafter, the attempt to use acupuncture as a means of birth control was abandoned.

Can Acupuncture Be Used For Abortion?

The Chinese seem to have tried every possible use for acupuncture. Around 1960, several hospitals in Shanghai initiated experimental programs to induce abortion through the use of acupuncture treatments and the taking of herbal medicine orally. Although there were a few successful cases, the results were not encouraging enough to warrant further research.

The ancient classic literature has repeatedly warned that pregnant women should not receive acupuncture treatment on the Hugu and Sangingcio points because it would result in a miscarriage. However, when abortion was desired, miscarriage would have been considered a blessing rather than a disaster. In 1979, the *Journal of Traditional Chinese Medicine* reported that 300 pregnant women in China who requested abortion were given acupuncture treatments on the acupoints mentioned above. They waited, but the results were quite disappointing. This illustrates the fact that the ancient Chinese classics of medicine were not completely free from errors. However, acupuncture treatment can induce uterine contraction, induce and shorten labor time as well as reducing labor pain.

Can Acupuncture Treatment Be Used To Prevent The Flu?

The *New Chinese Medicine* (March 1958) published an article about experiments conducted in China during a flu season at a school with 1,055 students. The experiments confirmed that moxibustion treatment as a method of preventing flu yields favorable results. When a flu epidemic hit the school with a 38% rate of student absenteeism, 272 students were administered moxibustion treatments daily before school while an almost equal number were not given the treatments. After three days, flu continued to hit the control group while only one student from the treated group came down with the flu. After the fourth day, the treated group was already immune to the flu, while it continued to infect the control group in up to 97% of the students in some classes.

In another experiment done in China, 818 persons from a community were chosen to receive moxibustion before the flu season. As a result, none of the 818 came down with flu, while a sizeable percentage of the other people in the community did. In Japan, where acupuncture is quite popular, it is also often used to combat diseases or flu. It was reported that in 1937, some school areas in Japan even required all students to show scars (resulting from moxibustion) on certain acupoints before they could be admitted to school. In the West, such a requirement would be contested in the courts.

Is Acupuncture Helpful For Attaining Longevity?

The ancient Chinese medical classics made numerous recommendations about administering moxa treatment on the Zusanli, Guanyuan, or Qihai acupoints to achieve longevity. One ancient book said, "if you want to be healthy, do not let the Zusanli point be unattended." Another said, "Don't travel with people who do not adminster moxa treatment on Zusanli." In both China and Japan, there are many citations about people who self-administered simple moxibustion treatment to attain longevity, and it is still being done by many Chinese and Japanese. This heat treatment (without needles) can be learned within minutes and can be self-administered safely.

In *Methods of Moxibustion,* by Xie Xiliang (San Xi, China, 1984), a legendary story is told about why the Japanese people like to administer moxibustion to attain longevity. During the rule of De Chuan Mu Fu (1542-1616 A.D.) it was customary to have the oldest person cross a bridge at its opening ceremony. On one occasion, Wan Bingwei was invited to cross a new bridge in Tokyo during the opening ceremony. General De Chuan was very impressed by the old man's age and asked what in particular the man had done to attain such longevity. The old man replied, "It is not difficult. In my family, we administer moxibustion on the Zusanli point every day for eight days at the first of the month, every month without fail. I am 174 years old, my wife is 173, my son is 153, and my grandson is 105."

Can Acupuncture Treatment Help To Prevent Stroke?

It may. There are ancient Chinese medical classics that claim moxibustion treatment administered on the Zusanli acupoint can prevent stroke, but few acupuncturists pay any attention to it. This may change in the future because of the research discovery presented by Jiang Youguang at the Second National Acupuncture Symposium (1984). Jiang and his associates conducted two studies to determine the effects of moxibustion on patients who had hypertension with cerebral thrombosis during the convalescent period. The objective indices of these studies were the plasma fibrinogen and fibrin degradation products (FDP). It is known that elevated levels of plasma fibrinogen or FDP can cause cerebral apoplexy (stroke). Patients in these two study groups were administered ten moxibustion treatments with two- to three-day intervals between.

The first group of 56 patients was examined for plasma fibrinogen and it was discovered that twenty-five of them (44.6%) had elevated levels of fibrinogen (400 mg% and above). Moxibustion treatments significantly reduced the elevation while little or no change was discovered for those whose levels of fibrinogen were normal in the beginning.

The second study involved 60 patients who had hypertension and were examined for FDP levels. Forty of them (66.7%) had elevated levels (above 20 r/ml). After ten moxibustion treatments, there was a remarkable decrease in FDP ($P < 0.05$), and the effects persisted even six months after the moxibustion treatments.

Thus, the researchers concluded that moxibustion treatment on the Zusanli acupoint may offer some protection against stroke for those who have hypertension combined with elevated levels of plasma fibrinogen and/or fibrin degradation products.

Can Acupuncture Treatments Be Used To Combat Cancer?

There are sporadic reports in Chinese medical journals that acupuncture treatments can be used to combat some types of cancer. However, there have been so few case reports of this kind that it is just not feasible to draw any conclusion at this point in time.

What Is An Electric Stimulator?

An electric stimulator is a device that produces low-amperage electricity that can be connected to acupuncture needles already inserted in the body in order to provide extra stimulation. The current is capable of producing the same results that can be accomplished by continuous finger manipulation of the needle. The advantages of the electric stimulator are of course apparent. The stimulator is capable of providing stimulation to many needles at the same time, which is more than the fingers can do.

Who Invented The Electric Stimulator?

Dr. Louis Berlioz of France was the person who first conceived the idea and wrote about his concept in 1816. As acupuncture was little known and practiced even less in France at that time, there was no clinical application of the method until 1825, when another Frenchman, Dr. Sarlandiere, actually used it in clinical settings. The widespread use of the electric stimulator did not come about until after E. A. Goulden of England published his method of the use of it in the *British Medical Journal*. It was this publication that actually stirred interest in China, Japan, and some European countries to use the device in clinical practice.

When the Chinese were trying to advance acupuncture anesthesia in the 1960s, they soon discovered that good anesthesia results could be achieved when the needles inserted were stimulated continuously. Furthermore, they also found that when an electrical stimulator was used, manual stimulation was no longer needed. This provided scientific proof that the stimulator was in fact useful. That discovery prompted the Chinese to produce many kinds of stimulators for various uses. Today, it is difficult to find an acupuncture clinic without an electric stimulator.

Is It Essential To Use An Electric Stimulator To Achieve The Best Treatment Results?

No. Plain needle treatment is still capable of achieving the best results. The stimulator is helpful in some cases, but it is not always essential for good treatment.

Does Acupuncture Work On Animals?

Acupuncture also works on animals. This fact is not new, as it can be traced back to 1000 B.C. The book *Beh Luo Acupuncture,* compiled in the seventh century A.D., was the earliest existing publication on animal acupuncture.

The most comprehensive book on animal acupuncture is the *Horse Therapy,* compiled in 1608 A.D. by two brothers, both of whom were well-known veterinarians. The *Horse Therapy* was the most comprehensive book on animal acupuncture at that time, and to this day it is considered to animal acupuncture what *Neijing* is to acupuncture for humans.

Are There Any Independent Acupuncture Research Establishments In China?

Yes. Small acupuncture research establishments are numerous in China. They can be found in every province and major city, most of them associated with medical colleges and major hospitals. Besides these, there are two major research institutes, one in Shanghai and one in Peking. According to *Health News,* published in Peking (August 9, 1984), the Acupuncture Research Institute in Peking is the largest one of its kind. Since its establishment in 1951, it has developed into a well-equipped research institute staffed by 2,274 full-time persons, 86% of them scientific researchers. There are 13 research departments covering such fields as the physiology of channels and collaterals, biochemistry, anatomy, acupuncture theory, and clinical practices. The departments are further subdivided into subject areas, with an outpatient clinic that sees two to three hundred patients daily.

CHAPTER NINE
Patients' Testimonies

This chapter contains testimonial letters from patients who had acupuncture treatments and responded very positively. The letters were chosen from many and represent the best responses. The reader should thus not misconstrue these results as typical for anyone with a given ailment who receives acupuncture treatment.

Can Acupuncture Treatment Help A Person Stop Smoking Or Drinking?

Yes it can. It is a very good method to stop smoking or drinking, and the pain involved in this kind of treatment is among the least that can be experienced. Benefits of the treatment are twofold: First, it can remove the craving to smoke or drink. Second, it can prevent the withdrawal symptoms such as irritation, nervousness, depression, or loss of energy. After a successful treatment(s), the craving to smoke or drink will diminish while at the same time, tolerance for nicotine and liquor will be very low for a few days or longer, depending on how well one responds to the treatment(s). Smoking or drinking shortly after the treatment will make one sick.

Is Acupuncture Treatment Good For Weight Control?

Acupuncture treatment is a fairly good method for weight control although the success rate is not very high. About one person in four will not respond to the treatment. Among those who do respond, some will require occasional treatments to maintain the weight loss. A successful weight control treatment will enable one to experience the following:

(a) The reduction of appetite, making it easier for the person to control what and how much to eat rather than being controlled by the appetite, that is, wanting to eat most of the time.

(b) The capacity of the stomach to hold food will be reduced, and the person will feel full much sooner. Overeating will inevitably lead to stomach discomfort or vomiting until excess food in the stomach is out.

(c) Many will experience a diminished craving for sweets.

(d) In some people, body metabolism will be raised.

The following letter from a patient is related to smoking and weight control.

I am writing to express my thanks to you for all you've done for me and for my friends. I visited you back in October in order to quit smoking. I had smoked 2-3 packs a day for 30 years, and had tried to stop, but couldn't on my own. I haven't touched another cigarette since my visit. Your clinic was referred to me by friends and I have since sent 8 people to see you for smoking or weight loss, all of whom have had great success.

I traveled from Louisiana to come to your clinic and am glad I made the trip. It paid for itself the first month with the money I saved on cigarettes.

I wish you much success in the future. Thank you again.

Bobbie Gordy

Can Acupuncture Treatment Help Nerve-Related Problems?

Yes it may. The following letter reveals an unusual case history.

I am a grocery store worker. In early May of 1982, about one o'clock in the afternoon, I suffered a shoulder injury resulting from chasing and fighting with a shoplifter when I tried to recover thirteen pounds of meat [from him]. Because of the should pain, I was receiving medical care constantly since the injury, but it went nowhere. Instead of getting better, it became worse.

After three months, the shoulder (right side) problem spread to the right arm. At first, I had only numbness in the arm, then, about another three months later, my right hand went to sleep and I lost the feeling in my entire right hand except the palm. I reached a point [where] the existence of my right arm could only be verified by (1) touching it with my left hand and (2) by visual assurance. This strange situation was made even worse by the feeling that my right palm was always hanging somewhere in the air beside my body. Although the existence of [my] right palm could be felt in some kind of a phantom situation, I was continuously perplexed and hounded by the feeling that it was a palm belonging to somebody else, yet it was attached to my body in a very mysterious way. I felt I was being hounded by this mysterious palm wherever I went. The loss of feeling in my arm was also accompanied by the loss of function of it. I just could not direct or move my hand to do things I wanted. The worsening situation led my doctor to send me to the hospital just before Easter 1983. I spent one week in the hospital, and the tests and treatments gave no relief. One of the three doctors suggested operation on the vertebrate (3rd to the 5th). After lengthy discussion with my wife, I decided against it at that point in time. As there was nothing the hospital could do, I was released. I was even more depressed with the problem when my friend, Mr. Lee, alerted and introduced me to you.

When I came to see you, you gave me no assurance that the problem could be treated by acupuncture but [said] you would try. The first acupuncture treatment on the vertebrate, on April 18, 1983, gave no help at all and neither did the second treatment show any sign of relief. When the [third] treatment was shifted to the arm, the four needles inserted on my upper arm brought immediate results. I experienced 40% recovery of the feeling in my right hand during the treatment.

The best result was achieved during the 6th visit, with moxa heat treatment on the leg. During that treatment 80% of the lost feeling was recovered. After that, the recovery was speedy and steady and after about ten treatments, my problem was all over. I am grateful to you for solving my problem without any operation.

Paul Chan

Can Acupuncture Treatment Help Resolve Acid Indigestion Problems?

Yes it can, and the results can be pretty good, as seen in the following letter.

Fifteen years ago, I started to suffer from heartburn and acid indigestion. Whatever food I ate, indigestion followed. The nervous stomach created gas, a lot of gas, and without medicine, every hour was like hell. When it was severe, I could not sleep, not to mention heartburn, which was also most unpleasant. Though I had been through many kinds of tests and x-ray, nothing had helped, and the only thing I could do was take medicine three times a day and every day.

Then, in early August of 1984, my wife suddenly suggested [I] try acupuncture, as I would try anything that might help. I went to you for just two treatments, and to my surprise, these treatments worked like a miracle. I stopped taking medicine right after the first treatment, and not only was I right away free from indigestion, I have been able to eat anything I want. I really feel it is a pleasure to be able to enjoy food again.

Cicero Guerra, Jr.

How Long Does It Take For Acupuncture To Work?

As mentioned earlier, it may take quite a few treatments to see results for some chronic problems. But there are many diseases or problems for which acupuncture treatments can yield immediate results. The letter below provides some examples.

I am a 60 year old nurse (R.N.). I have had various problems which Dr. Ling has treated.

First, I was treated to quit smoking and it has been about two years since I quit smoking. While I was receiving acupuncture treatment to quit smoking, I also had [a] headache. Surprisingly enough, my headache was gone instantly when the first and only needle was inserted on my hand.

A few weeks later, I returned to the clinic for water retention treatment. I was asked to empty my bladder just before the treatment. With two needles and just after 15 minutes, I had to rush to the restroom again.

I had symptoms of nervousness and was also treated with immediate results.

C.C.

Can Backache Be Helped By Acupuncture Treatment?

Backaches of various kinds have a fairly good chance to be helped by acupuncture treatments. This, among many other acupuncture treatments, generates curiousity because people find it difficult to understand why needling on the hands has anything to do with back pain. The letter below is related to treatments for back pain.

It has been a year now since you treated my back pain and I am still doing fine. I want to write you this letter to thank you again, and to let other people know about what acupuncture has done for me.

I am a middle-aged woman. I was living in Chicago, working for a major company when I fell and fractured my left pelvis. Since then, severe pain developed in my back and leg. Needless to say, I started to see doctors for the pain problem. One doctor recommended spinal surgery while another disagreed. As months went by, I not only had no relief from the various treatments and drugs, my pain was becoming worse. At first, the pain pills temporarily stopped the back pain but after two years, I discovered that the pills were no longer effective. One doctor told me that the nerve damage to my spine and leg was permanent, that there was nothing that could be done for me, and that I must learn to live with the pain.

Three years after the incident, my left leg had a very "rubbery" feeling and the tingling in my left foot was driving me crazy. Because of the leg giving way every time I stood up, I had to wait a couple of minutes before I could start walking and then I was afraid my leg would give way again.

Around Labor Day of 1983, my back pain reached an intolerable point. I could not stand straight nor could I move around without being assisted. No pain pills could give any relief, I was completely exhausted, and I really felt I wanted to die. My daughter discovered you and requested emergency treatment on a Sunday afternoon in September of 1983. I was assisted by my daughter and son-in-law to your clinic, to try another method to relieve my pain. I encountered hope for the first time in four years. Most of the pain went away after the treatment and I could straighten my back and leave your clinic unassisted. When I came for the second treatment the following day, the pain was all gone, and I felt as though I had been reborn—the back pain was gone.

Today, more than a year after your treatment, I am still free from back pain and I want to thank you again for all you have done to relieve my pain.

Estelle McG

If A Patient Responds Very Well To The Treatment Of An Ailment, Will He Also Respond Very Well To Treatments Of Other Ailments?

Normally yes. The next letter explains that.

Before I went to see you, I suffered backache for 24 years. I tried everything I could but nothing had helped my backache. I remember I was having so much pain on the day I first visited you that my son had to help me into your office. But right after the first treatment, I had little pain left and I could walk away by myself without [a] problem. After I received two more treatments for my backache, all the pain was gone. It has been over a year now and I still have no backache. I am back fishing in my boat, riding my motorcycle, and many things more.

I received two weight control treatments from you and since then, I have lost 42 pounds and have maintained it.

I had bursitis for 6 years and could not raise my elbows any higher than my shoulders. In one treatment, and within three days, I could and have since been able to raise my arms without pain, and as high as I like.

I had constipation for at least a year and was using stool softener and other drugs. I have not used any drug since the treatment.

It was November of 1983 [when] I visited you last. I have been healthy and enjoy a good life. I [would] like to solicit for acunpuncture for the good health of my fellow man.

W. M. Johnson

Can Acupuncture Treatment Help Sinus Problems Or Arthritis?

Both arthritis and sinus problems are known to be treatable by acupuncture and with fairly good results. The letter below covers both.

My wife, myself, and our daughter all had sinus problems for twenty some years before we went to see you. Strangely enough, my daughter married somebody, also with sinus problems. All four of us had to take medication all the time, and with my daughter, it was like hell when the sinus hit her hard—terrible dripping, affecting her work at times. All of us came to see your for sinus and surprisingly enough, we all have no sinus problems after some treatments.

But by far the most astounding thing that I experienced was not the result of sinus treatments but that of arthritis treatment. I suffered arthritis on both of my hands and fingers for 30 years. In these 30 years, I could not get too much relief from medicine and I had to take pain pills just to be able to sleep. When I got up in the morning, I had to run hot water over my hands every morning before I could do anything. My hands had been very tight all these years and [I] could never make a fist. I remember during my second sinus treatment, I was also treated for arthritis in my hands with two needles on each hand. When those needles were withdrawn, I could immediately make fists with my hands, with no pain. I never dreamed such a thing could happen and I was thrilled with joy at that moment. After the treatment, the stiffness of the hands was gone and I could use my fingers freely and easily. After I came home, I did a lot of yard work, which I always like to do but [had] found very difficult because of the arthritis.

It has been a year and a half since we first came to see you and we all still enjoy the relief that you have given us. We would like to thank you again.

Jack McClure

Can Acupuncture Treatment Help Someone Suffering From Psoriasis?

Acupuncture treatment can help psoriasis problems although the success rate may not be very high. The acupuncture literature reflects a lack of cumulative case reports on treatments for this disease. Furthermore, the acupoints recommended to treat psoriasis have been inconsistent. More often than not, this disease remains a "hot potato" to many acupuncturists. The following is a thank you letter from a psoriasis patient for whom acupuncture treatments yielded good results.

I suffered from psoriasis for five years, from age 17 to 23. The disease brought me terrible itching on one hand, and embarrassment on the other. During the five years I had psoriasis, I had scaly splotches all over my body—on my hands, legs, ears, scalp, and private area. Some splotches were as big as a softball. The disease gave me physical discomfort with constant itching to the point that I had to scratch until it bled at times. The condition was so bad on my arms and legs that I had to wear pants and long sleeve shirts at all times. This almost created a state of insanity. I almost drove my husband insane.

During this five years, I spent about $7,000 trying to get some relief but nothing worked, and it kept on driving me crazy. I was on the verge of taking nerve pills when I tried another method—the acupuncture.

After Dr. Nancy Ling gave me the first acupuncture treatment, surprise came in just one hour. The psoriasis began to subside. In four days it was almost gone, and after a few follow-up treatments, I was free from that lousy psoriasis which had plagued me for five years. I feel wonderful now and my husband wants to join with me to express our utmost thanks for what you have done for us.

Debora Street

Can Acupuncture Treatment Help Someone With Knee Problems?

Yes it may. The letter below is from someone whose treatment brought fairly quick relief.

I want to thank you for the help and relief you gave me for my arthritic knee. As you well know, I was in a great deal of pain and limping very badly when I first sought your help. I had the problem for quite a while and all the help I sought could not give me any relief. The first acupuncture treatment gave me much needed relief and enabled me to walk normally. In fact, I had taken the elevator up to your office and after your treatment, I walked down the stairs without the excruciating pain that I had before the treatment. You gave me two follow-up treatments for the problem and I have had very little trouble with the knee since.

Since receiving my treatments, I have referred other patients to you for a variety of problems and they also have obtained relief.

Ralph J. Missere

For Those Who Respond Positively To Treatments For Pain, Do They Always Feel Better Right After The Treatment?

Usually they do, but once in a while, the patient may feel muscle soreness for a few days, after which relief will take effect. The following letter is a good example.

For eight years I suffered ever increasing pain in my tail bone area. Because I was pregnant at the time, and had two more pregnancies within the next three years, my doctors decided the pain was pregnancy related. After all three children were born and the pain increased in severity, it was felt that the problem was a chronic inflammation of my tail bone and it was aggravated by all the lifting and carrying (of children) that I did. I was on Naprosyn anyway, so the dosage was increased. However, the drugs did not, in any way, alleviate my pain. The pain attacks became more frequent and more severe. In December 1983 my rheumatologist x-rayed the area and discovered that my tail bone does a sharp L-curve into my body. He referred me back to my orthopedic surgeon (MD) to remove my tail bone. My orthopedic surgeon refuses to remove tail bones as dangerous and pointless surgery. For both this pain and for internal gristle-like scar tissue under my ankle, he referred me to Dr. T. Ling.

When I saw Dr. Ling in January 1984, the thought of living another 20 or so years (I was then 36) was depressing. During the pain attacks caused by my tail bone, I ceased considering myself as human. The pain literally left me incapable of thought. I endured, but not happily. The attacks generally occurred every 1-2 weeks, though often more frequently, and lasted anywhere from 20 minutes to 1½ hours.

The ankle tissue, which my orthopedic surgeon's only recourse was to surgically remove, was completely gone at the end of one treatment. There was unusual tenderness in the area for several days but since then there has been nothing—no scar tissue, no pain, no sensitivity.

The one treatment for my tail bone has literally changed my entire life. For about 7-10 days after treatment, my entire tailbone area was quite sore and extremely sensitive. About two weeks after treatment I had an attack that was just barely endurable. This was an exciting improvement. However, over the next three months or so, the attacks came less frequently and were of ever decreasing intensity. Now, almost 10 months later, the attacks occur only every four to six weeks and are so mild that I am only just aware of them. My life continues with no interruptions and no dread of the next attack.

Thank you from my whole family and especially from me.

Ruth B. Johnston

Can Acupuncture Treatment Help Someone Who Is Suffering From Shingles Or Post-Shingle Pain?

Yes. Shingles or post-shingle pain have a fairly good chance to be controlled by acupuncture treatments, and the best results can be achieved at the early stage when the blisters occur. As a whole, the earlier the treatments are administered, the easier to have them controlled. The following letter is from someone whose post-shingle pain problems we have been able to help.

I suffered from shingles around the left side of my head and my face with pain beyond what I could tolerate. It was so painful that I was admitted to the emergency room 3 times in 3 days and with not much relief. After a week or so, the blisters went away but not the pain, and it even created a problem for me just to sleep. As my neurologist could not help much, he found out about Dr. Ling and advised me to try acupuncture. I am very happy that I took the advice and tried acupuncture. The treatments helped reduce the pain during each and every treatment. I went to see my neurologist prior to my fifth acupuncture treatment and he was very pleased with the treatment results. After seven treatments, all the pain was gone, and I have since then been completely free from shingle pain.

Lately, someone in my neighborhood also suffered from shingles with blisters around the neck and on the head. Since her doctor only gave her pain pills to take, I referred her to see you while she still had the blisters. She is responding to the treatments even better than I did, and just after four treatments, all of her shingle pain was gone.

I would like to thank you again for everything you have done to stop my shingle pain.

Angelina Solis

Can Acupuncture Treatment Help Someone Who Suffers From Hypoglycemia?

Acupuncture treatment is known to be helpful to someone who suffers from such a disease. Here again is another letter.

What a difference your treatments for hypoglycemia have made in my life! For the first three treatments, I had to be driven to your clinic—65 miles from my home—by my daughter and required her supporting arm in walking from the car to the office because of physical weakness and disturbed equilibrium. For the 4th treatment my physical strength and courage had been restored to the point that I drove myself to keep the appointment.

Hypoglycemia, which is commonly referred to as low blood sugar, evidently is an imbalance of one's glandular reactions and can become quite devastating in reactions to sweets and carbohydrates as well as to stressful situations (my job as Museum Director is a demanding one). While the imbalances evidently are now corrected, I promise to continue eliminating all sweets and carefully consume a minimum of carbohydrates in my diet. Also to return to you for an occasional treatment even though I consider myself restored to vital health.

I wish to add an important thank you for relieving the carpal tunnel syndrome, which had been a very painful affliction of my right hand for the past several years. At this writing, the hand is completely relaxed and restored to its proper agility and without pain.

It is my experienced belief that acupuncture has a most important place in Holistic Medicine and Health—which is known to more and more of us as total health of body, mind, and spirit. I would be remiss if I did not state the obvious: that with the restoration of physical balance has come the renewal of my creative, mental awareness and spiritual attunement which gives great enthusiasm and joy in entering into every facet of life.

E.B.

About the Authors:

 Dr. Tiong-hung Ling and Dr. Nancy T. Ling grew up in a Chinese community in Asia. They both went to Vanderbilt University, Nashville, Tennessee, where he received his Ph.D. degree in Education and she acquired hers in Mathematics, shortly after they were married. They learnt acupuncture in Hong Kong and China. They have been practicing Chinese medicine for over twenty years in Houston, Texas, and treated patients from every state of the U.S. They both served as president of Texas Association of Acupuncturists (1994, 1995-98).